Jumbo Poop Emoji Coloring book for kids.

50 Pages of funny, Cute & Silly Activities for Children

Emoji Colors

Copyright © 2019 Emoji Colors

Designed by Freepik

greenthumbpublishing@gmail.com

I0465810

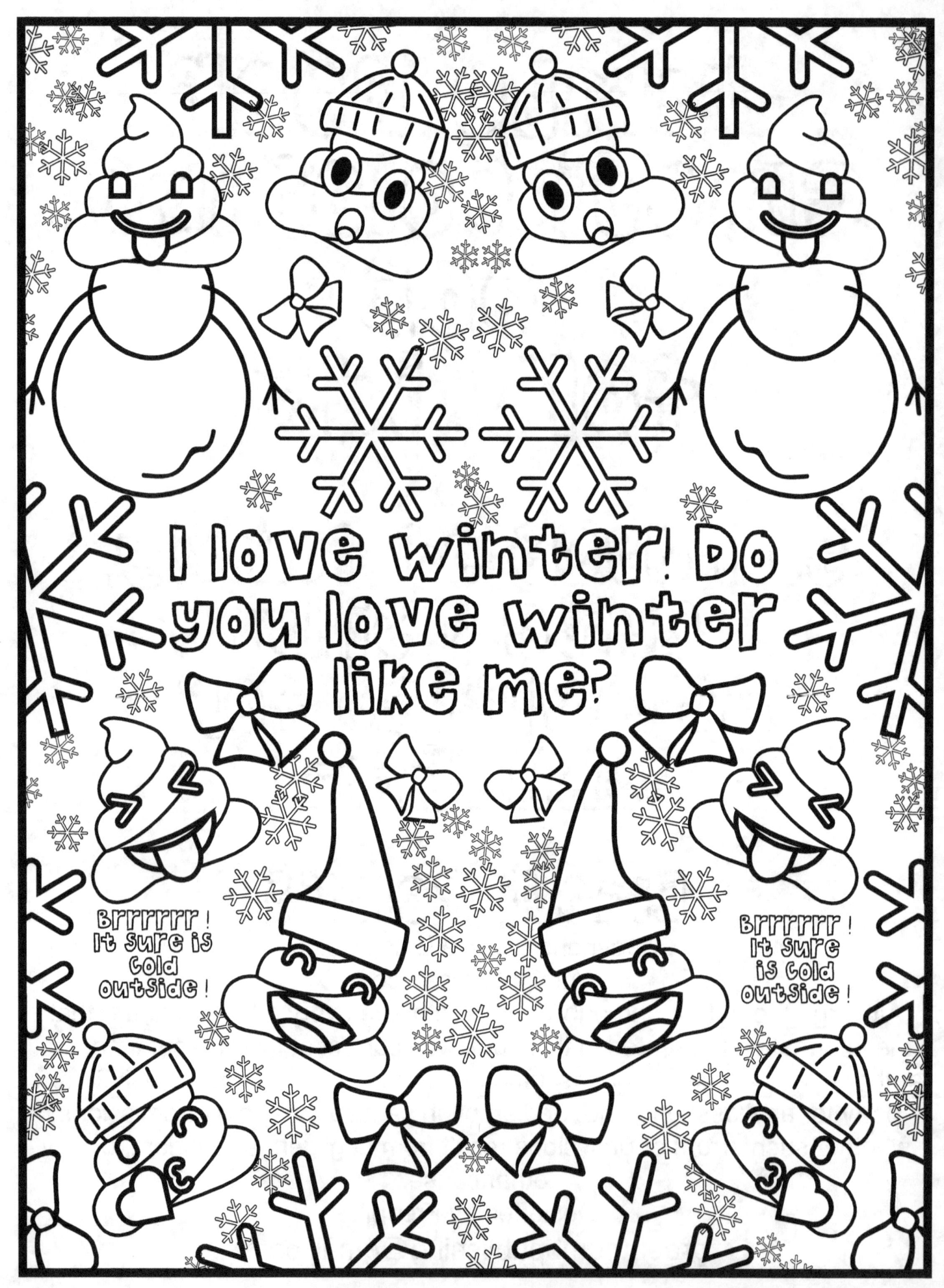

BLEED PAGE

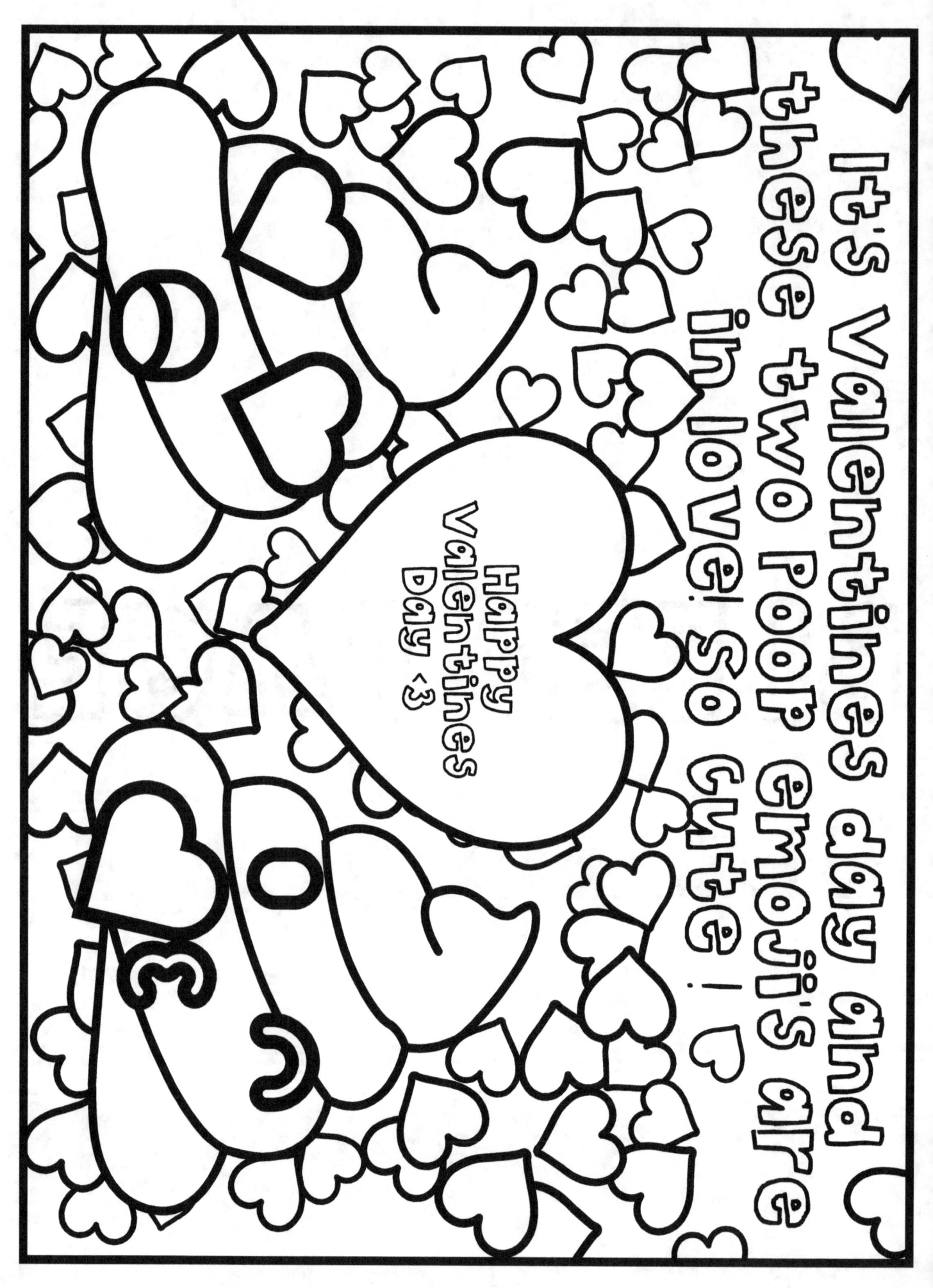

It's Valentines day and these two poop emoji's are in love! So cute!

Happy Valentines Day <3

BLEED PAGE

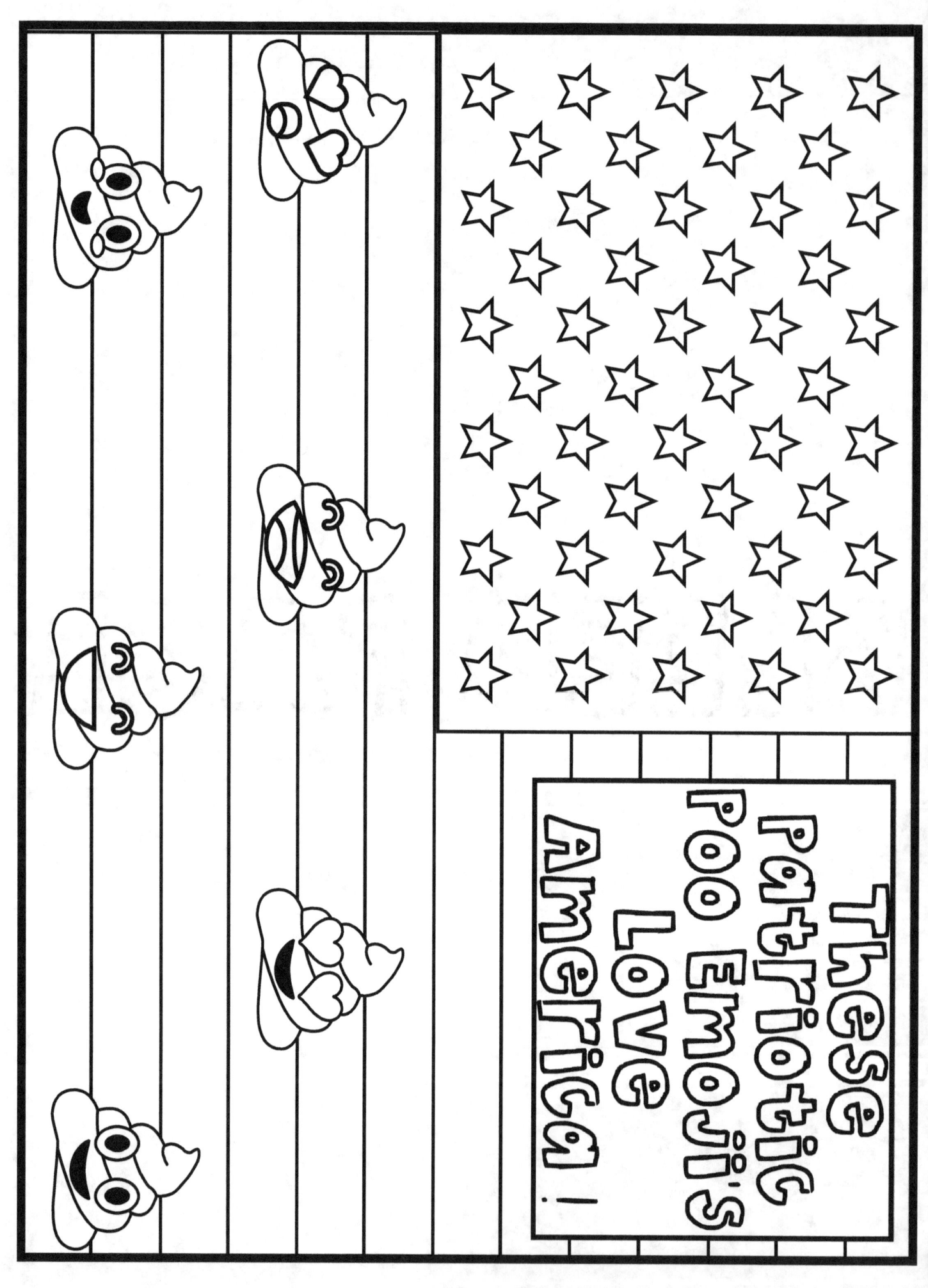

BLEED PAGE

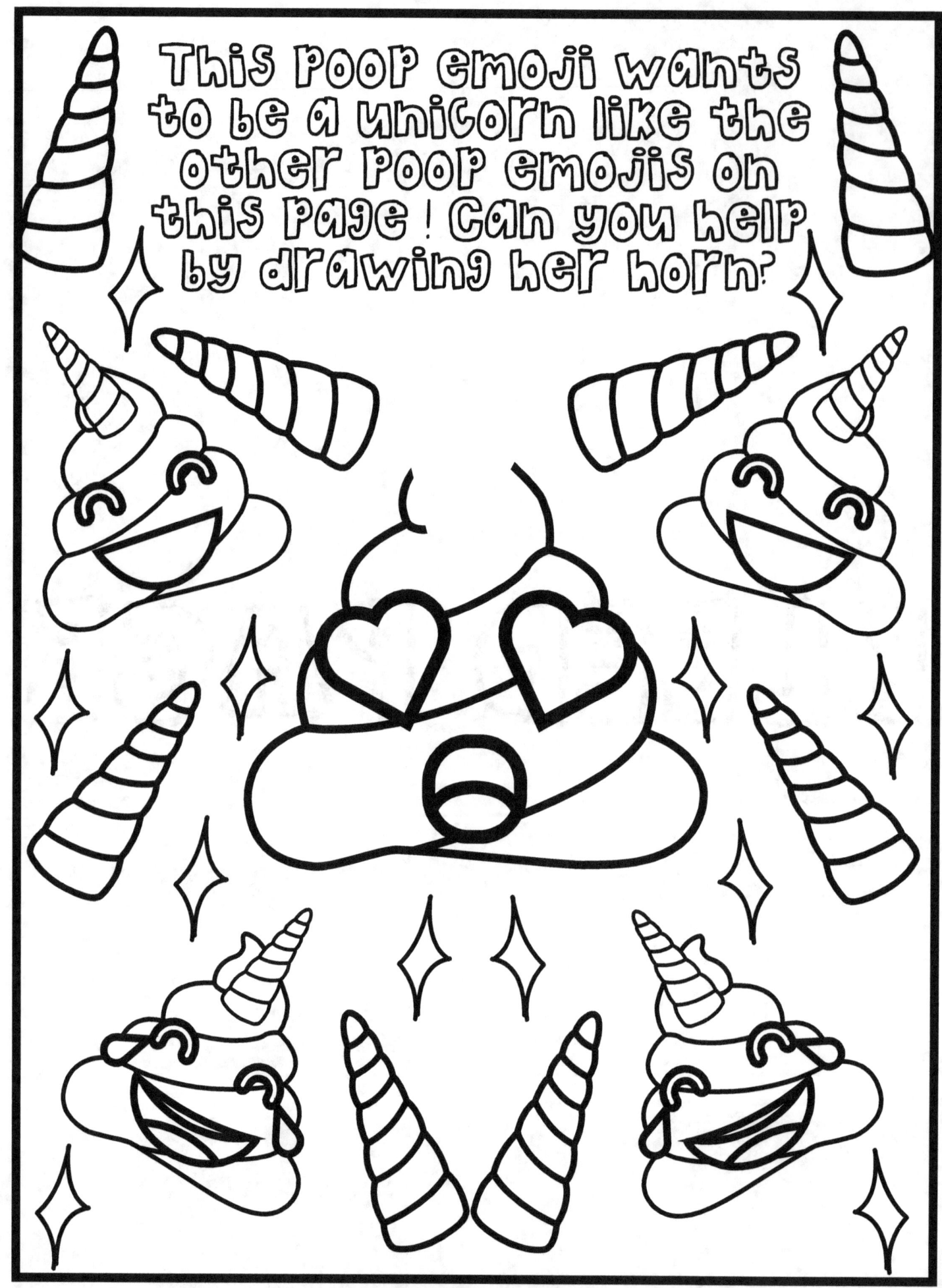

BLEED PAGE

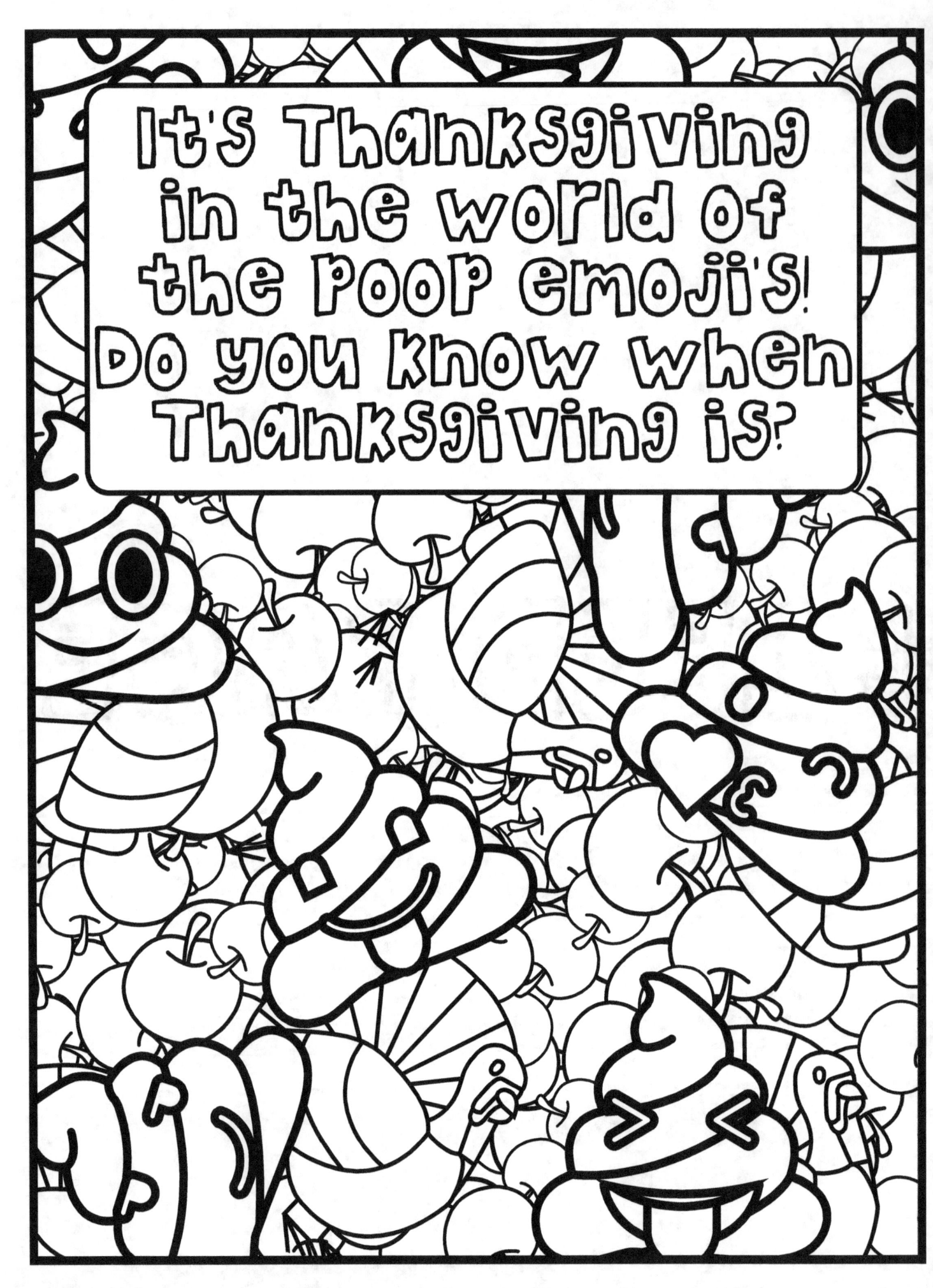

BLEED PAGE

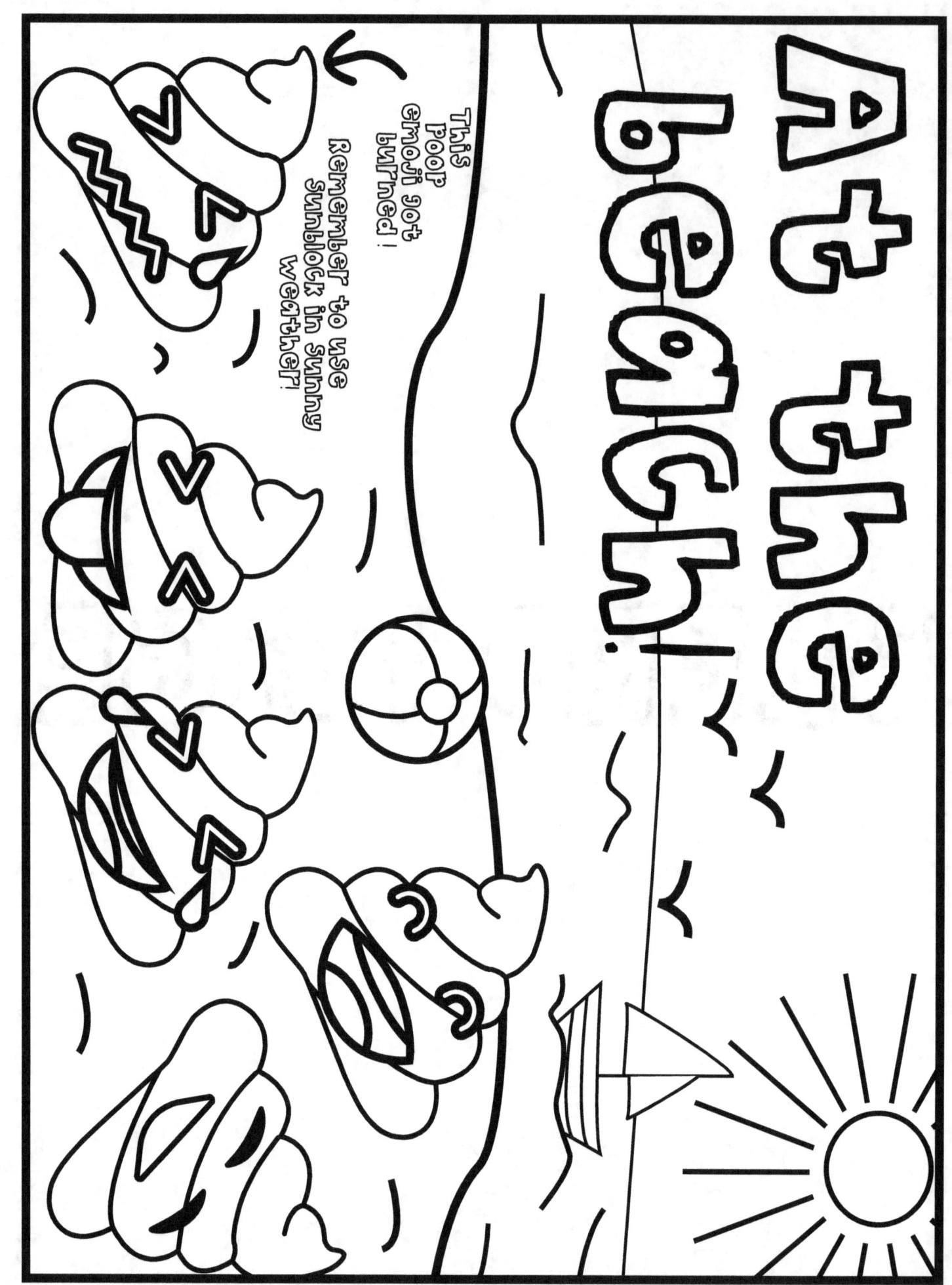

BLEED PAGE

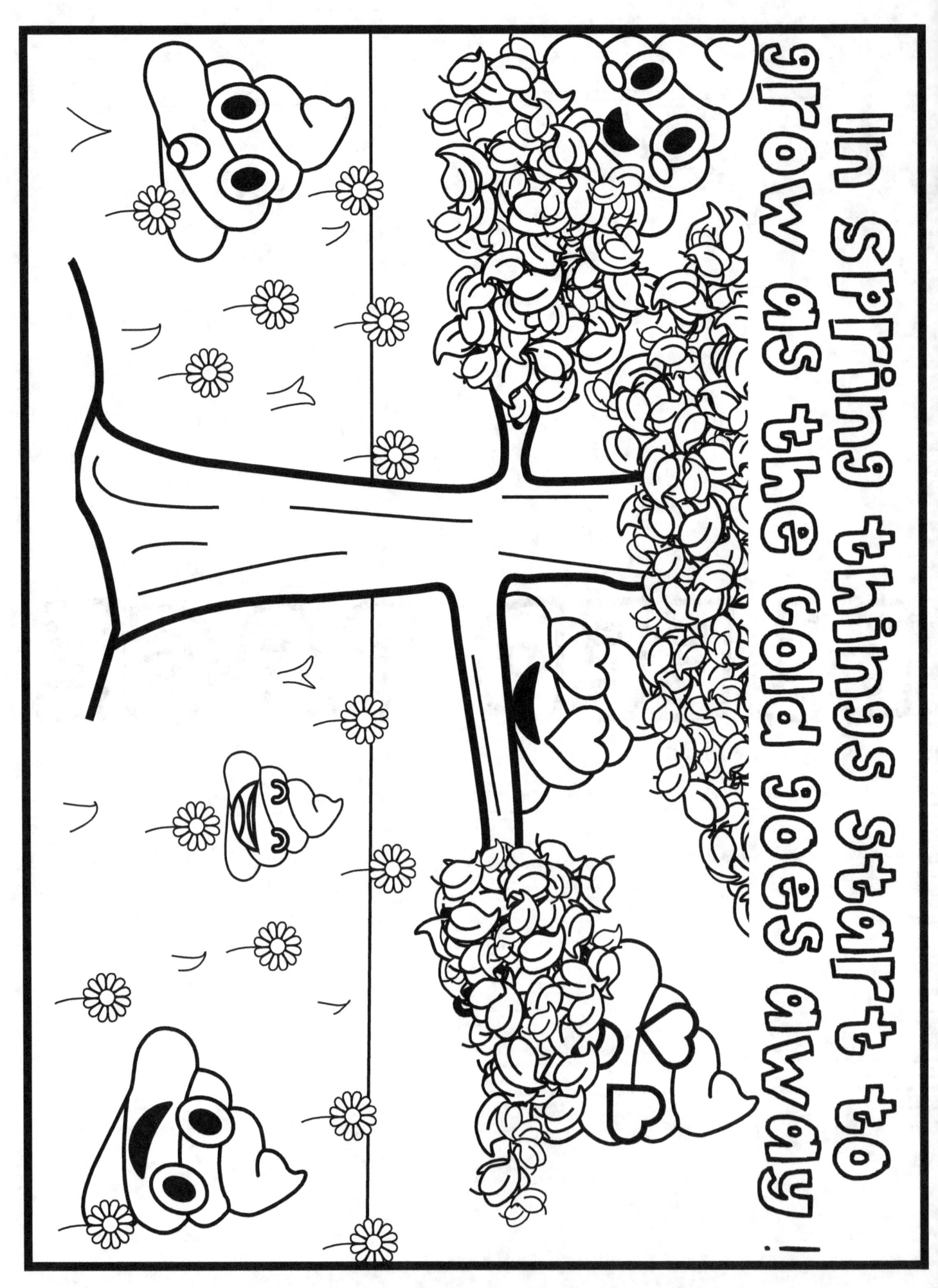

In spring things start to grow as the cold goes away!

BLEED PAGE

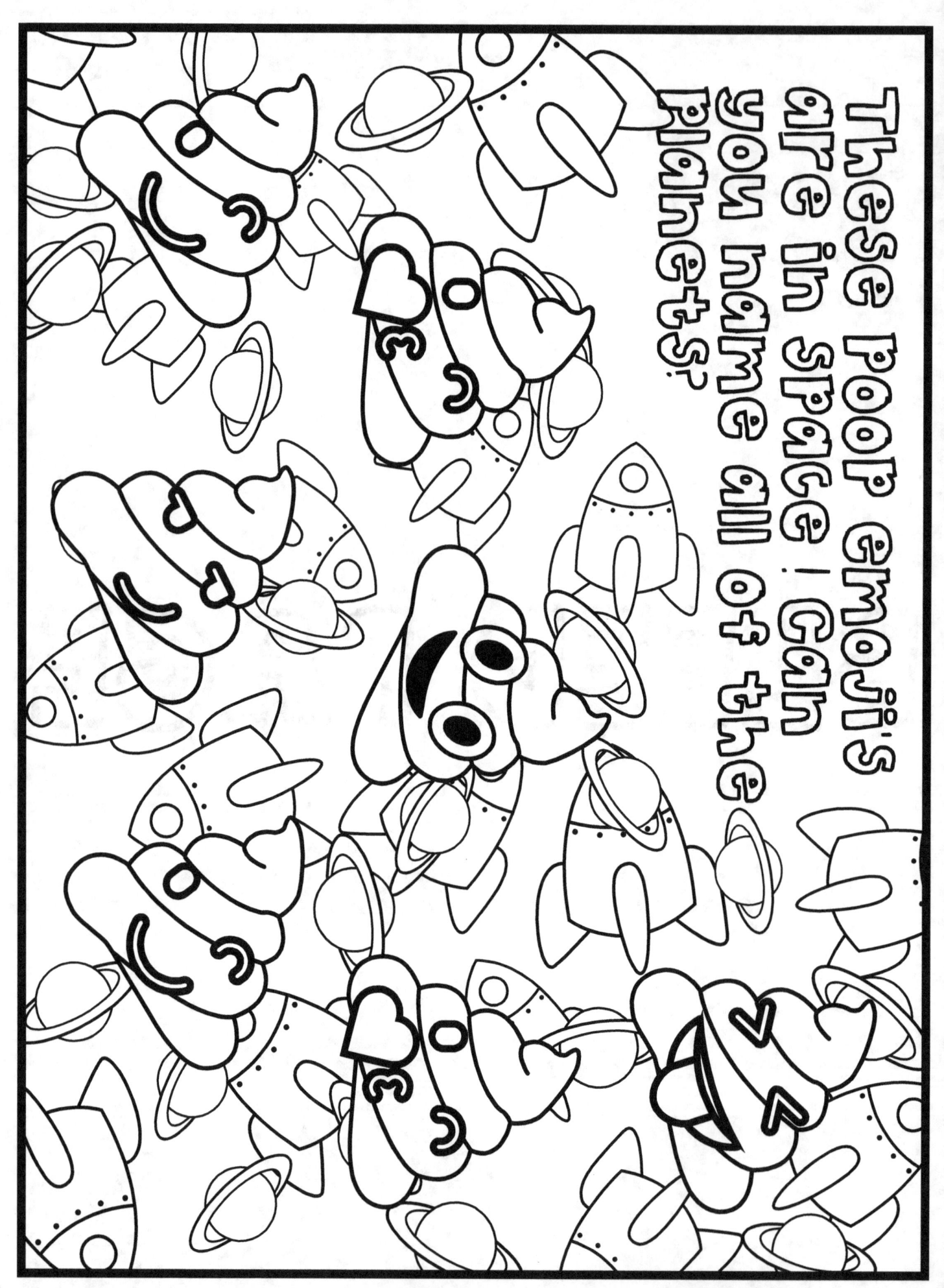

BLEED PAGE

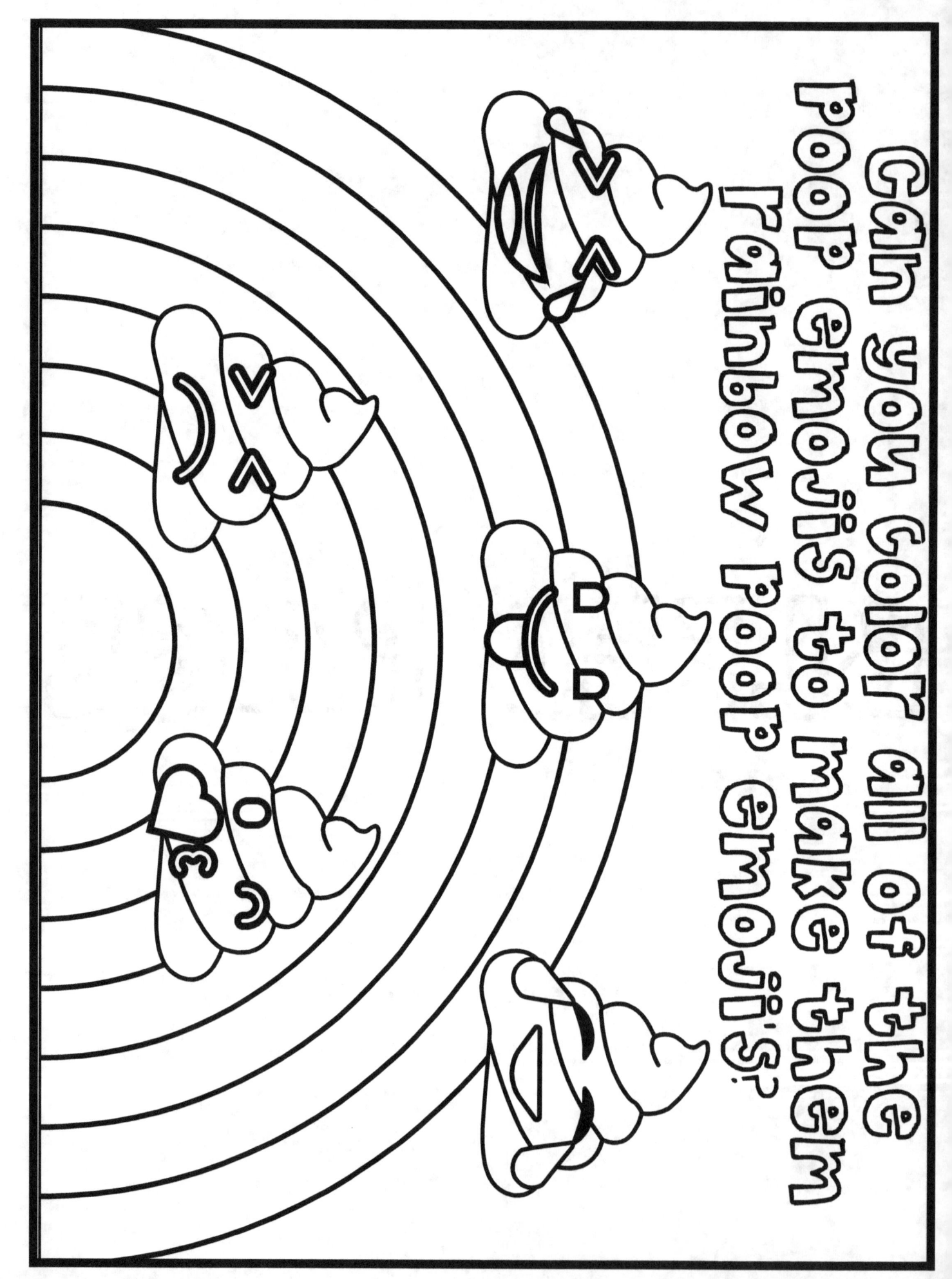

BLEED PAGE

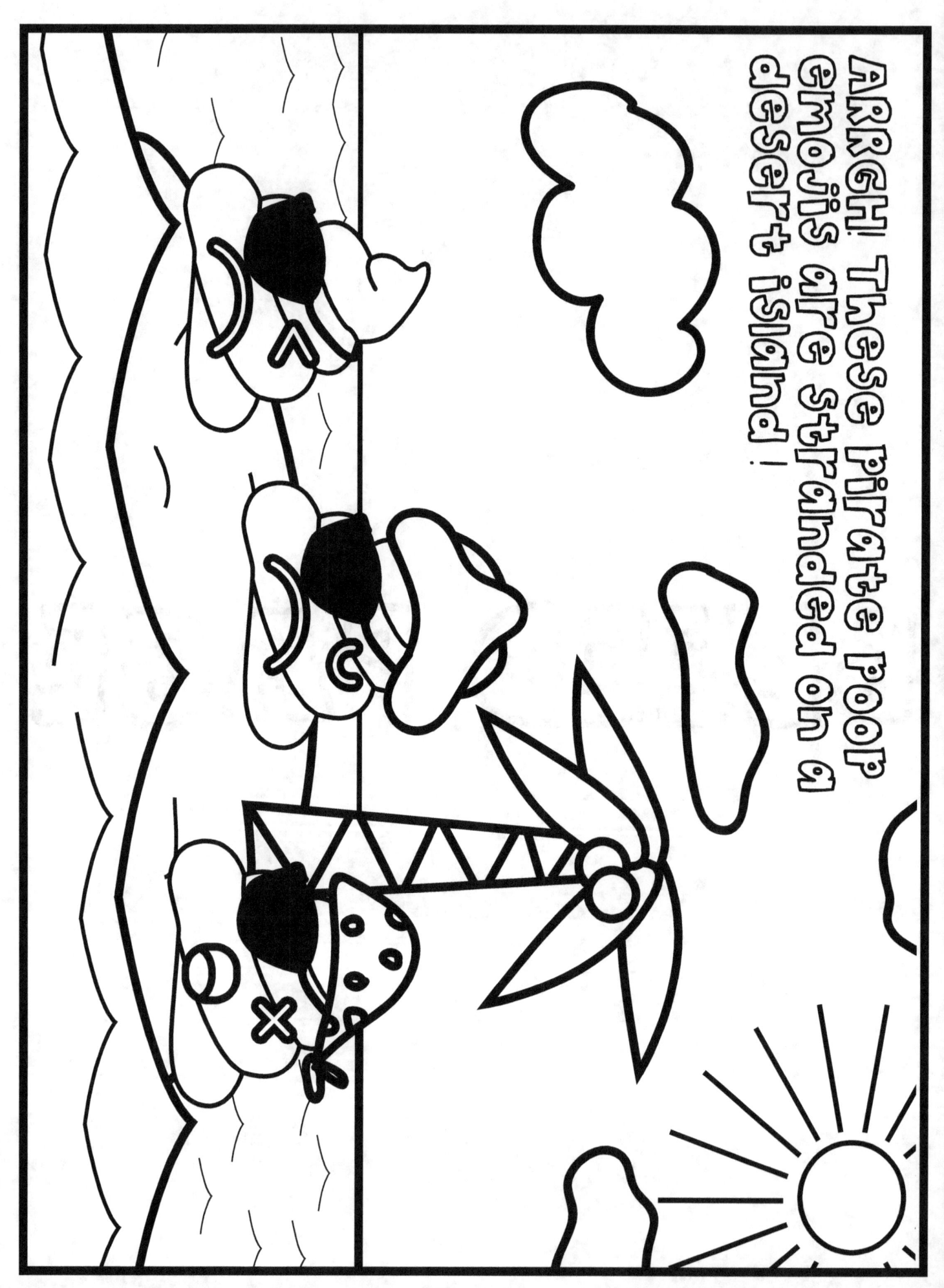

BLEED PAGE

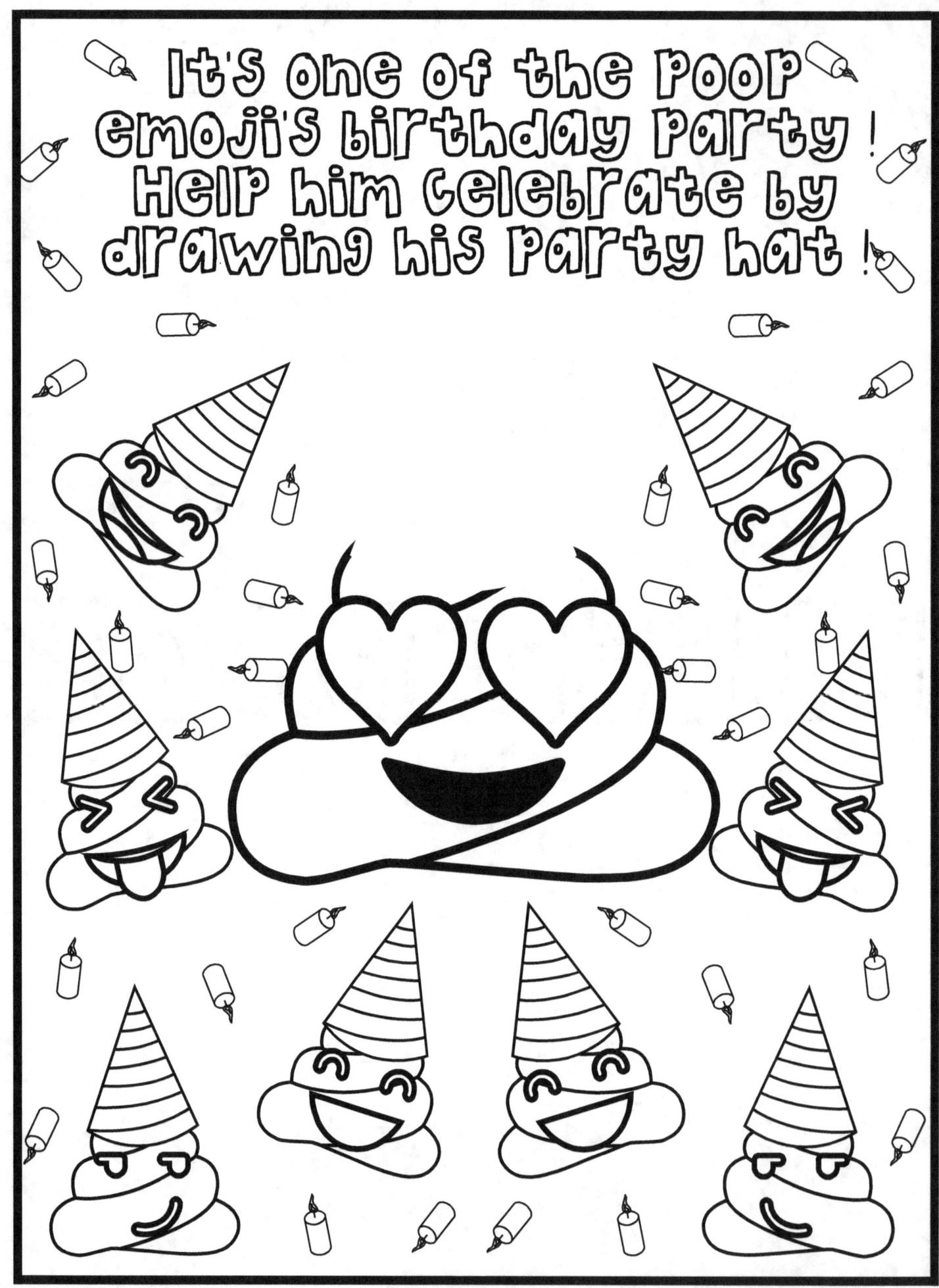

BLEED PAGE

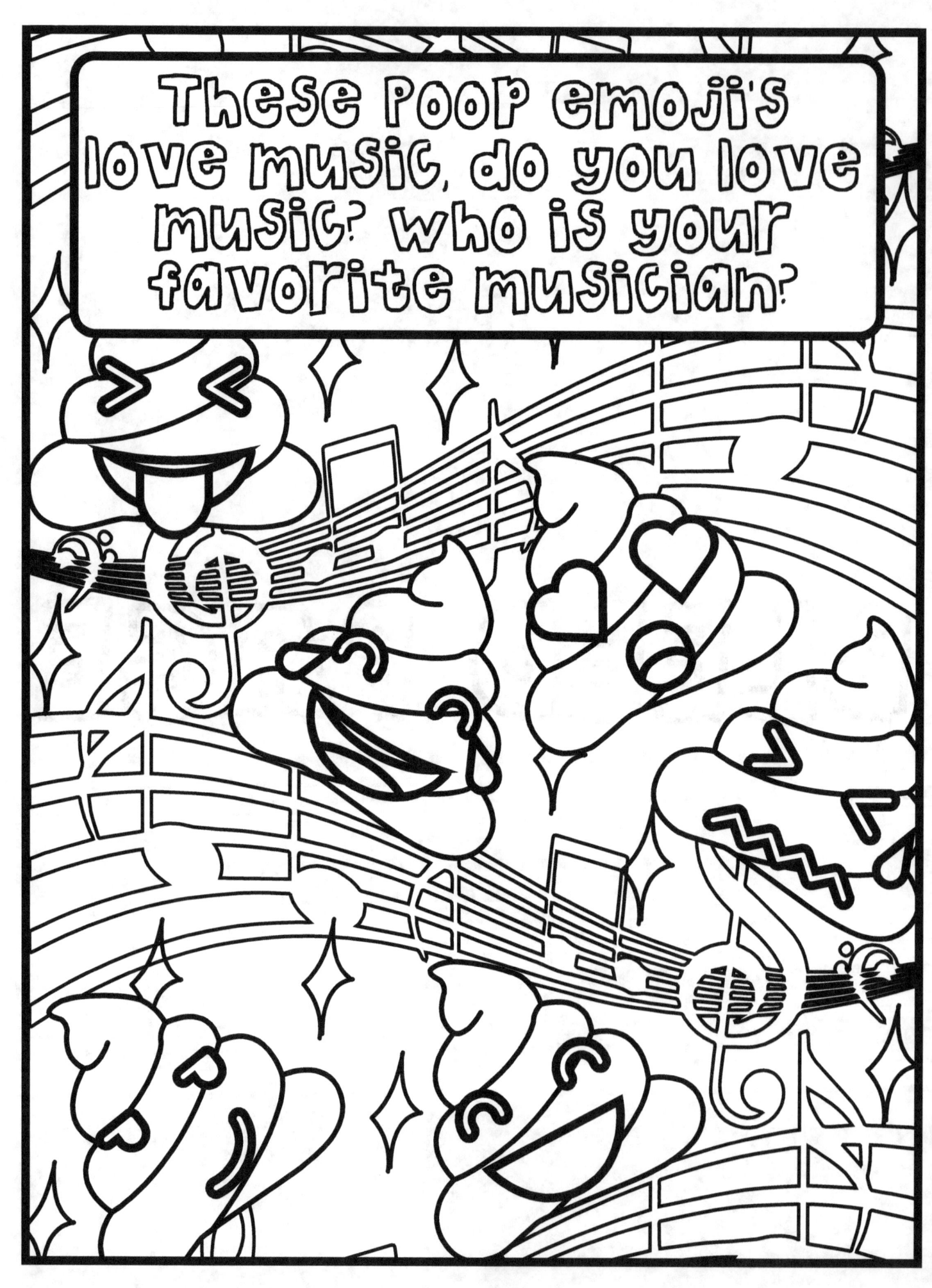

BLEED PAGE

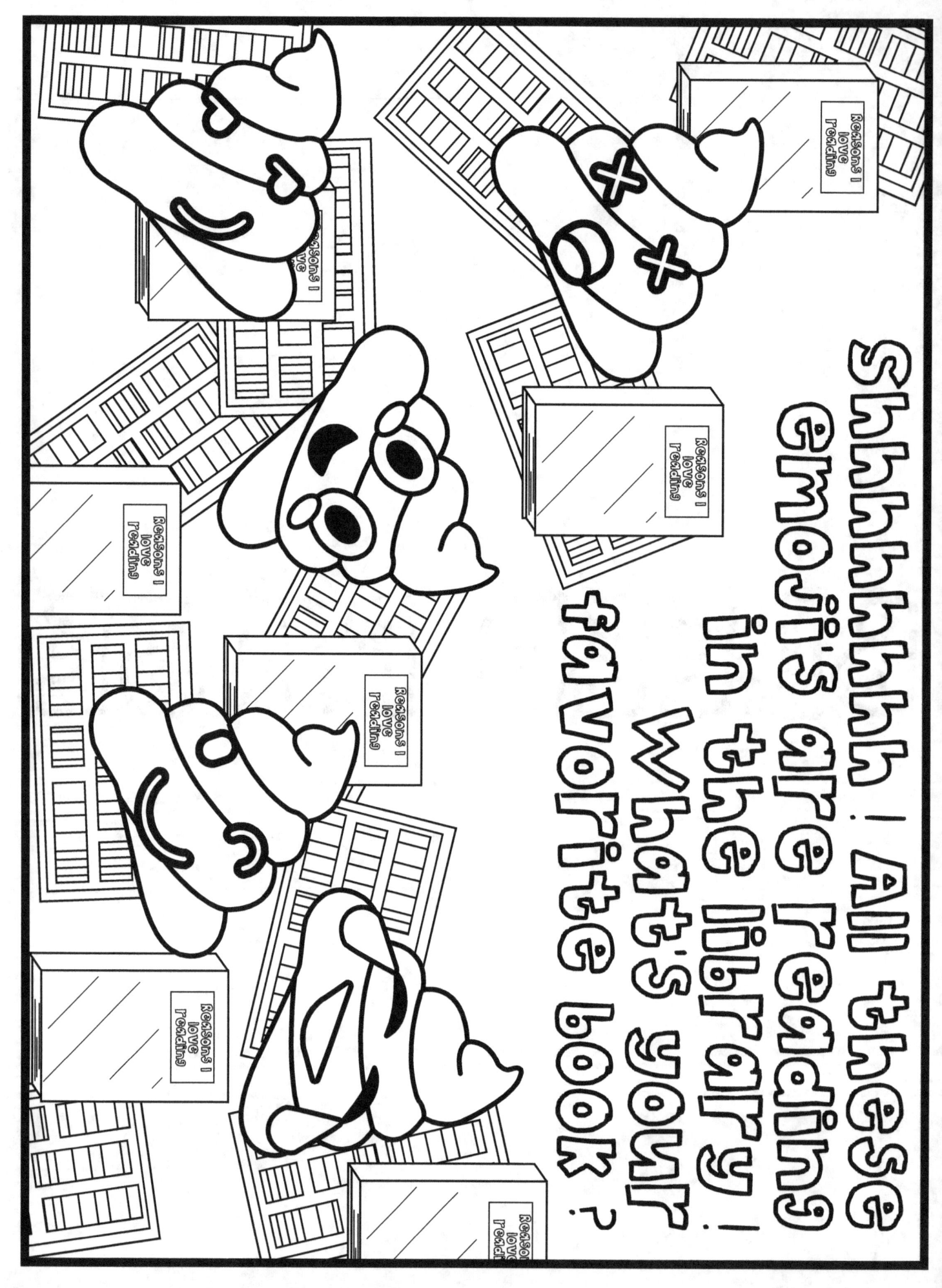

BLEED PAGE

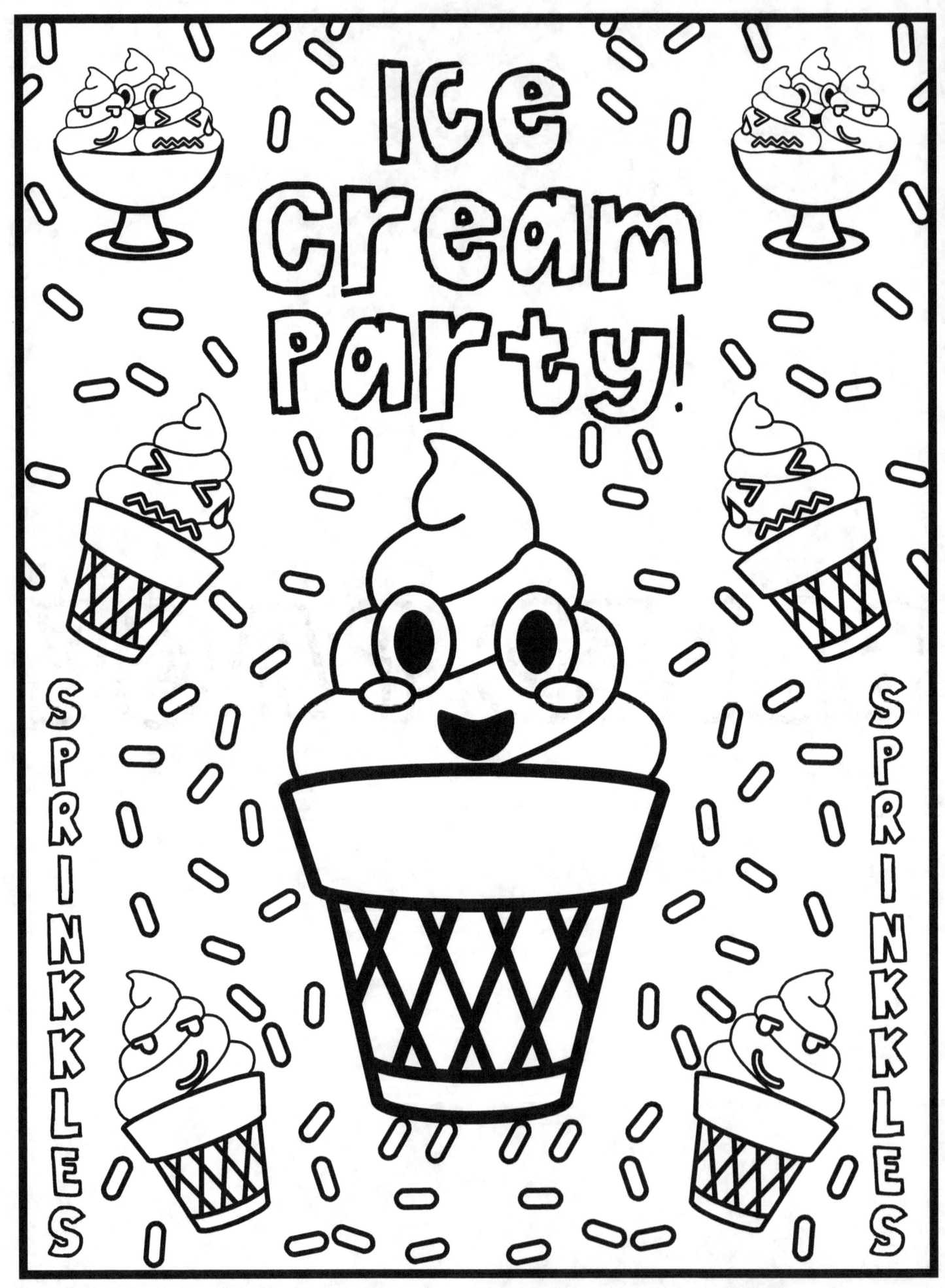

BLEED PAGE

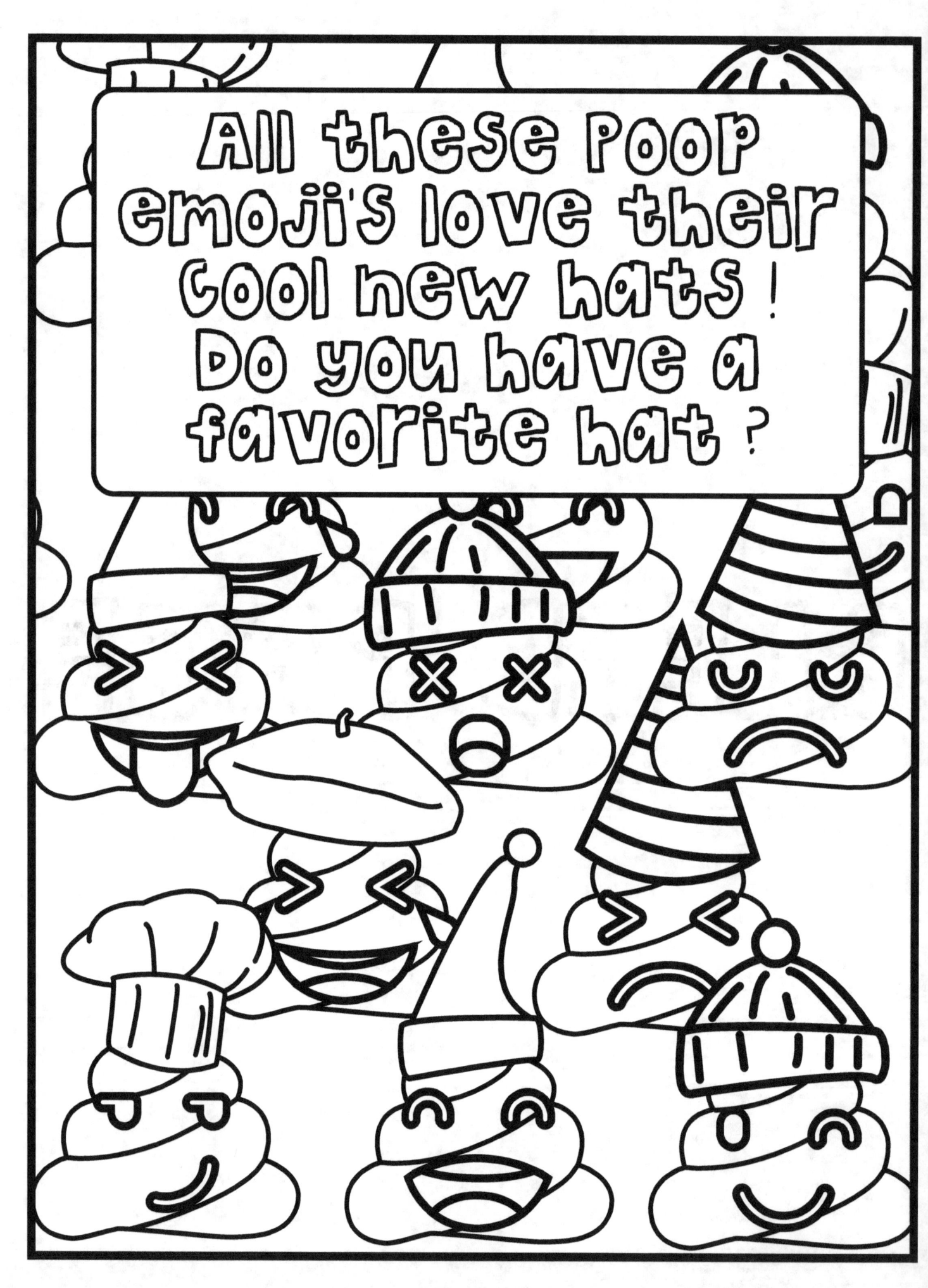

BLEED PAGE

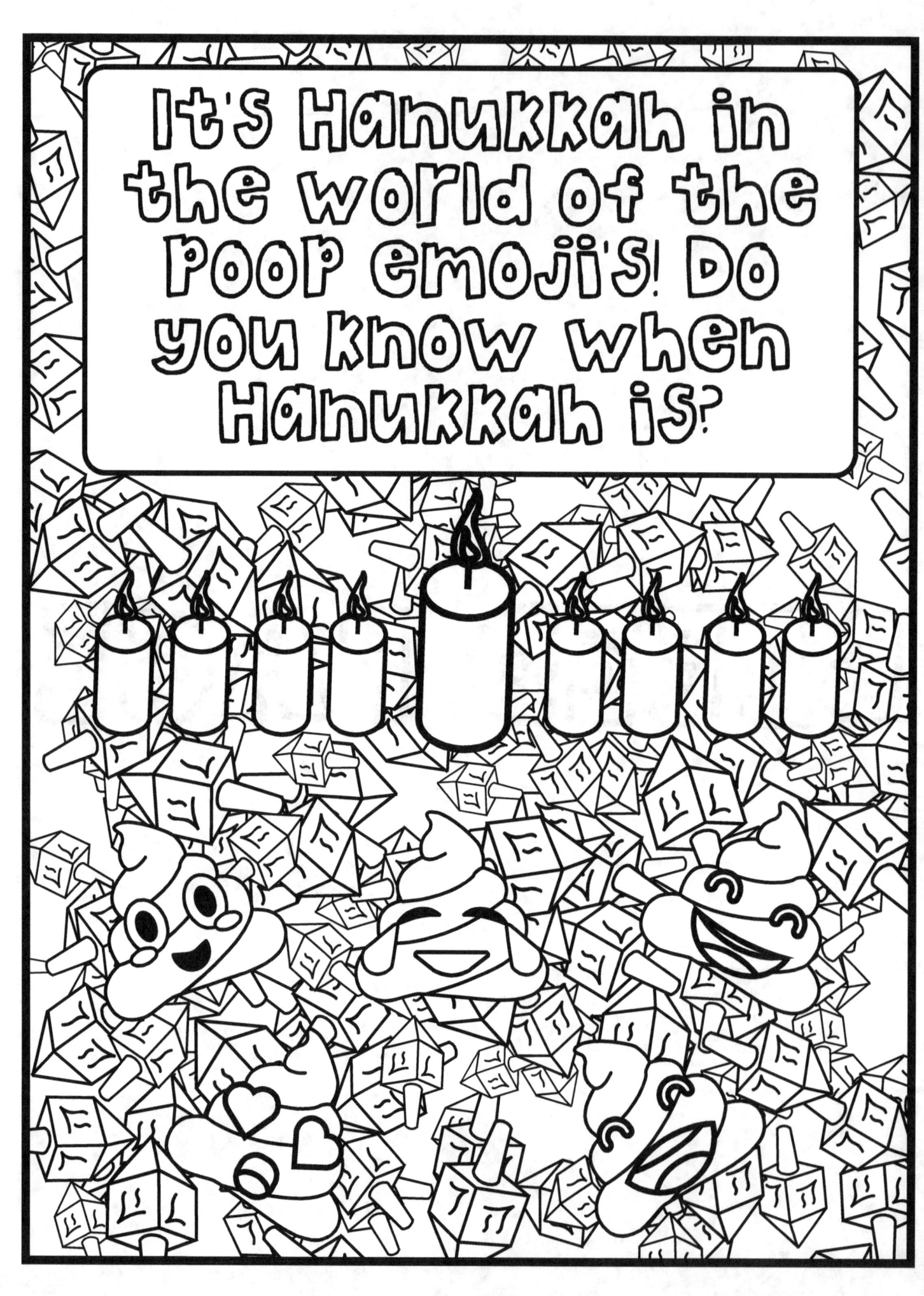

BLEED PAGE

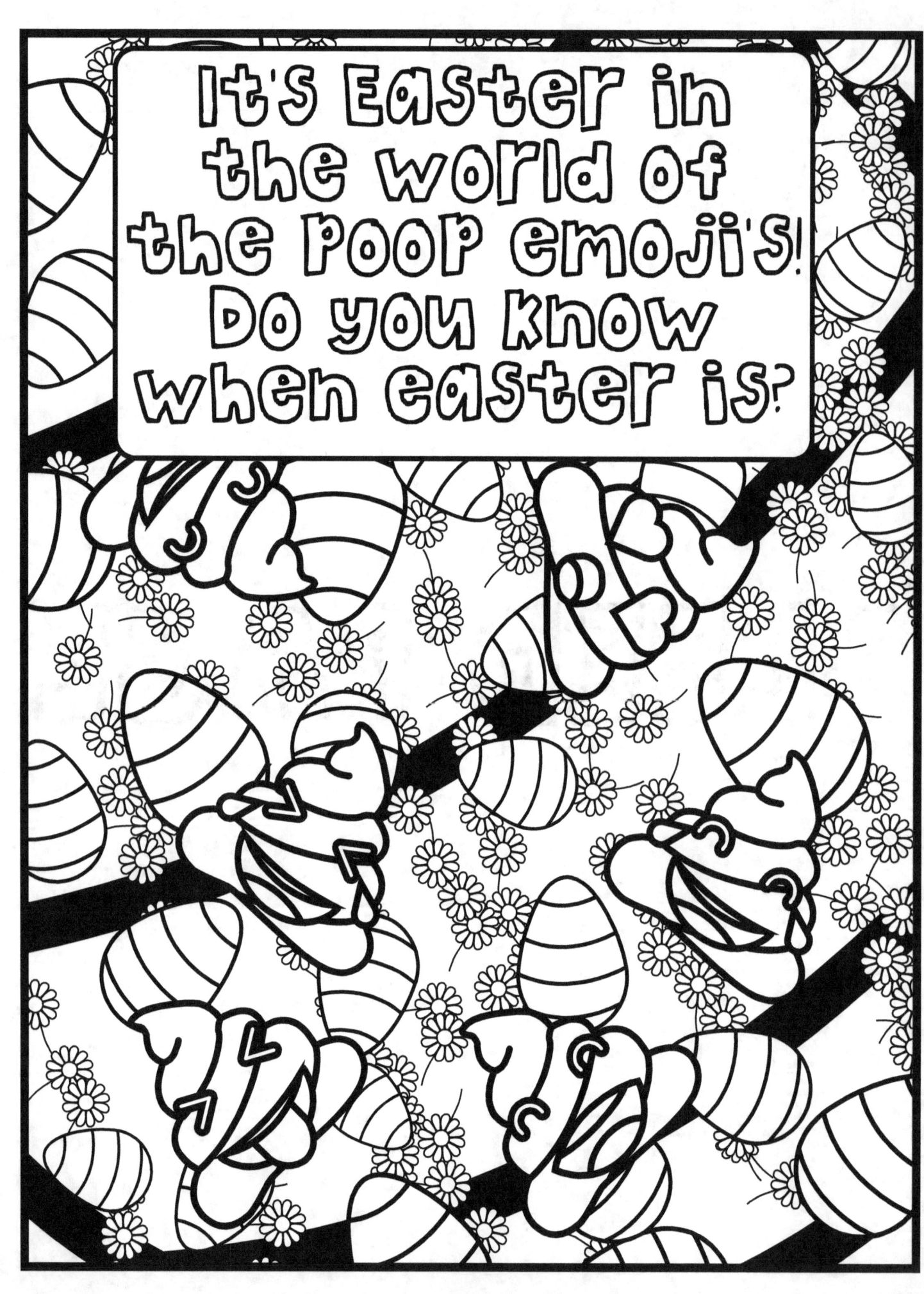

BLEED PAGE

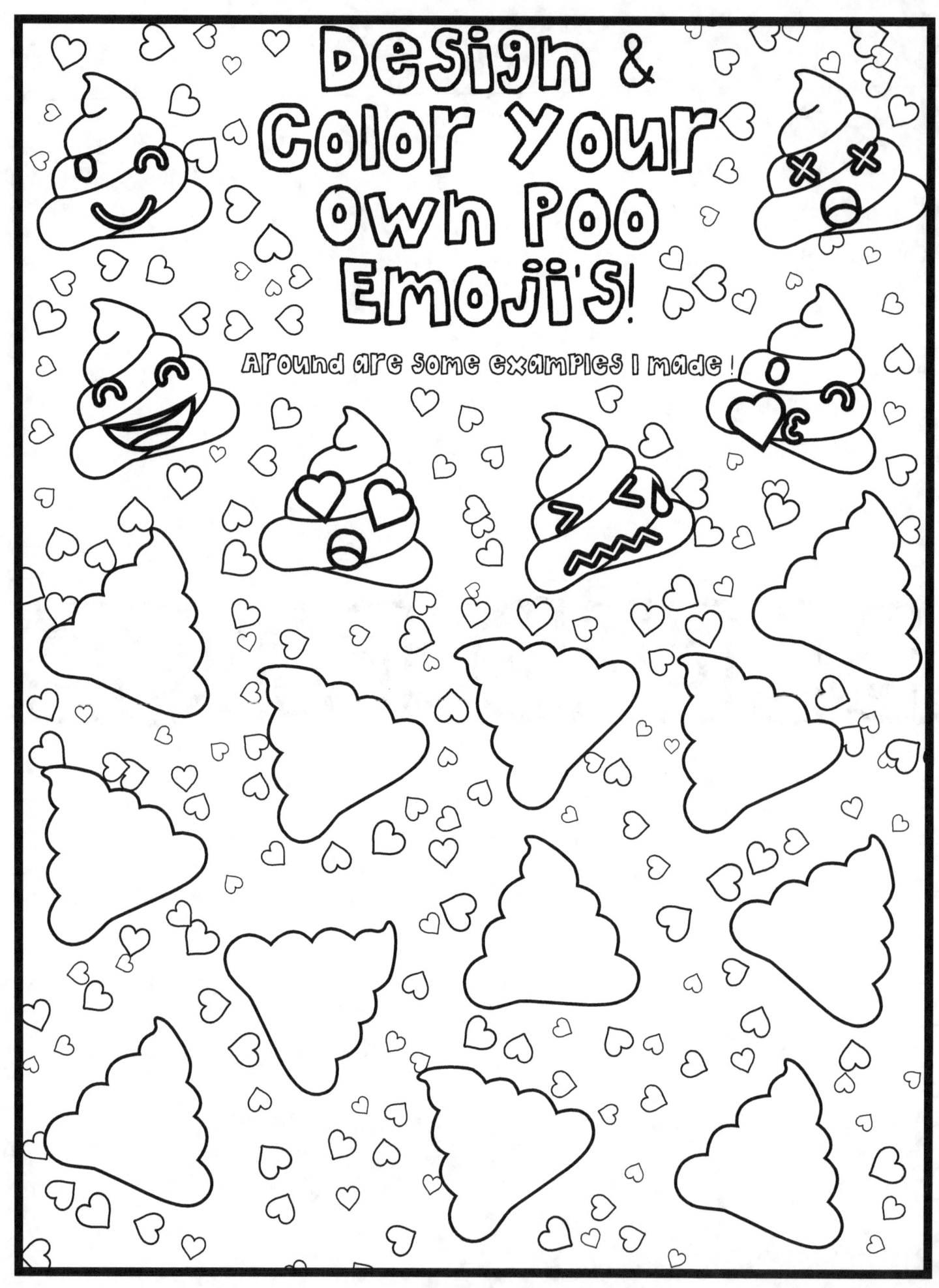

BLEED PAGE

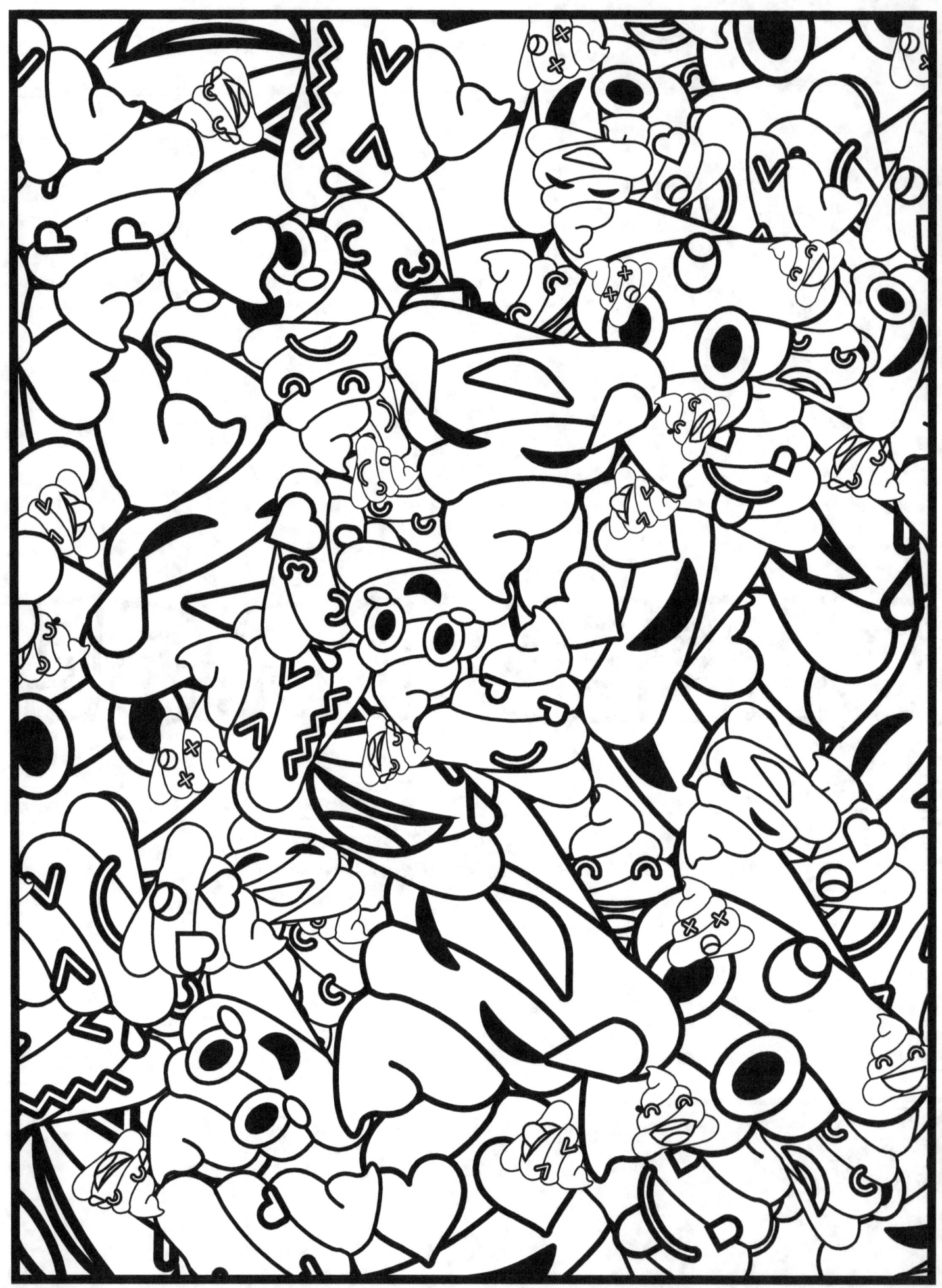

BLEED PAGE

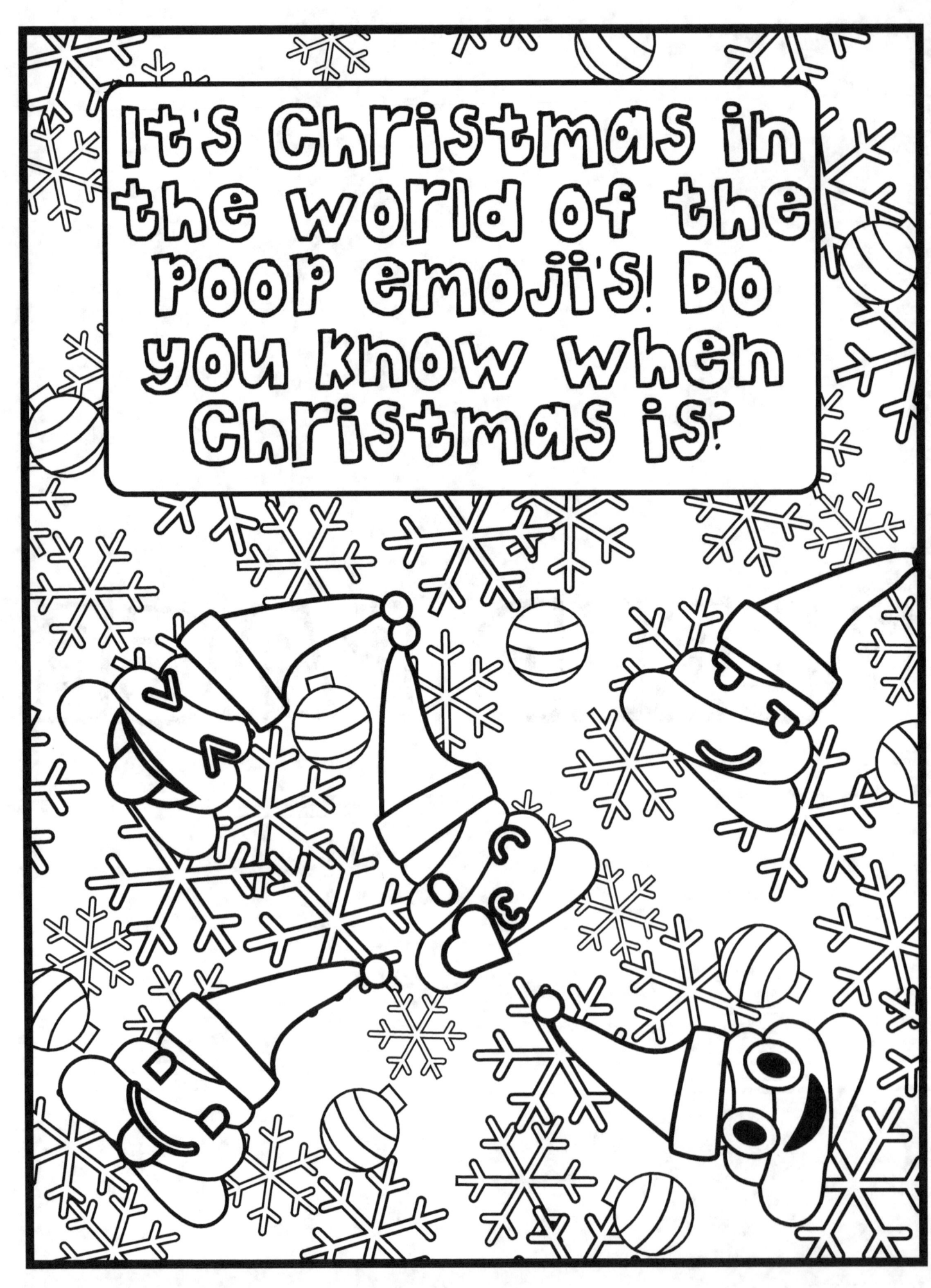

BLEED PAGE

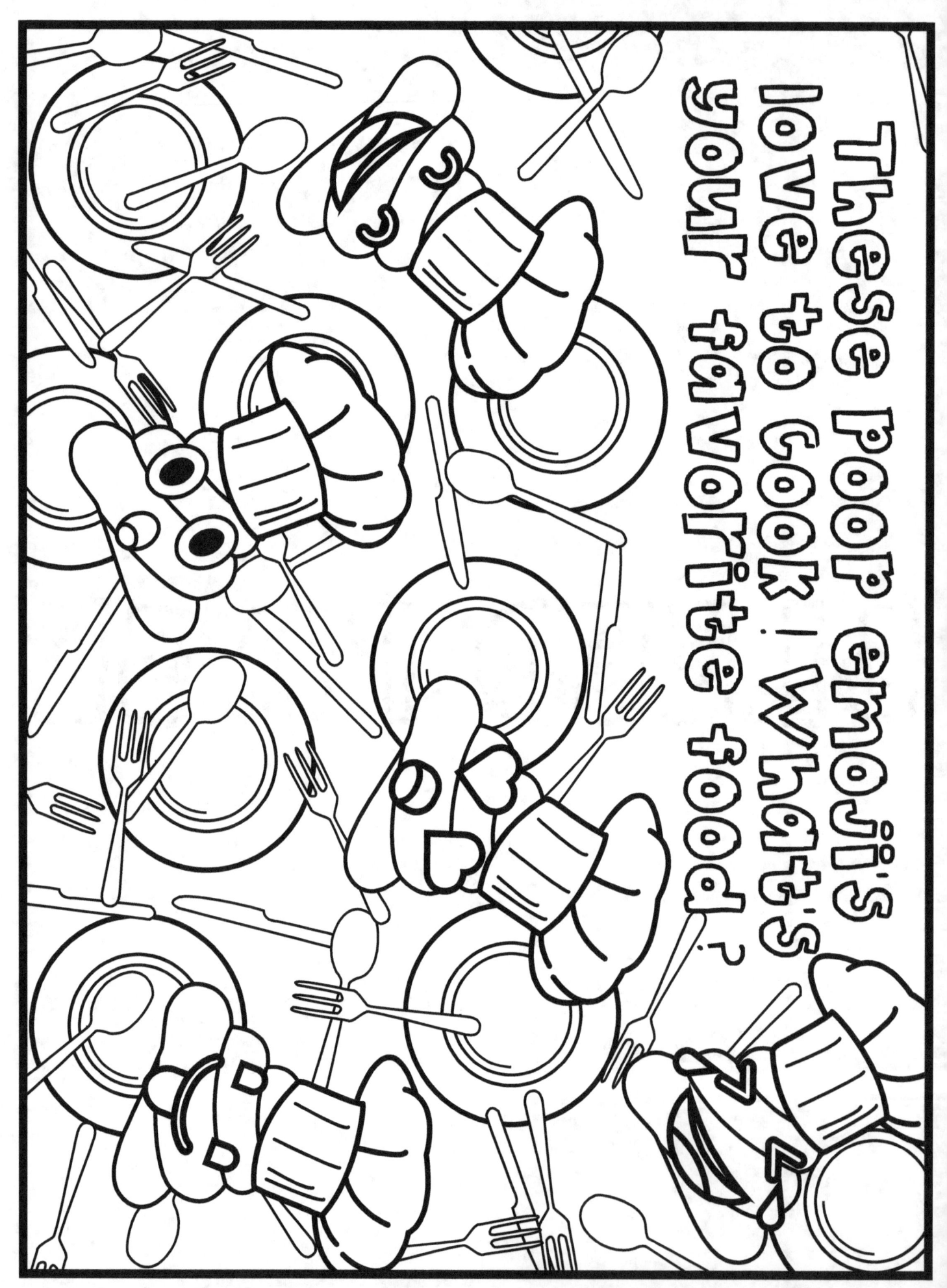

BLEED PAGE

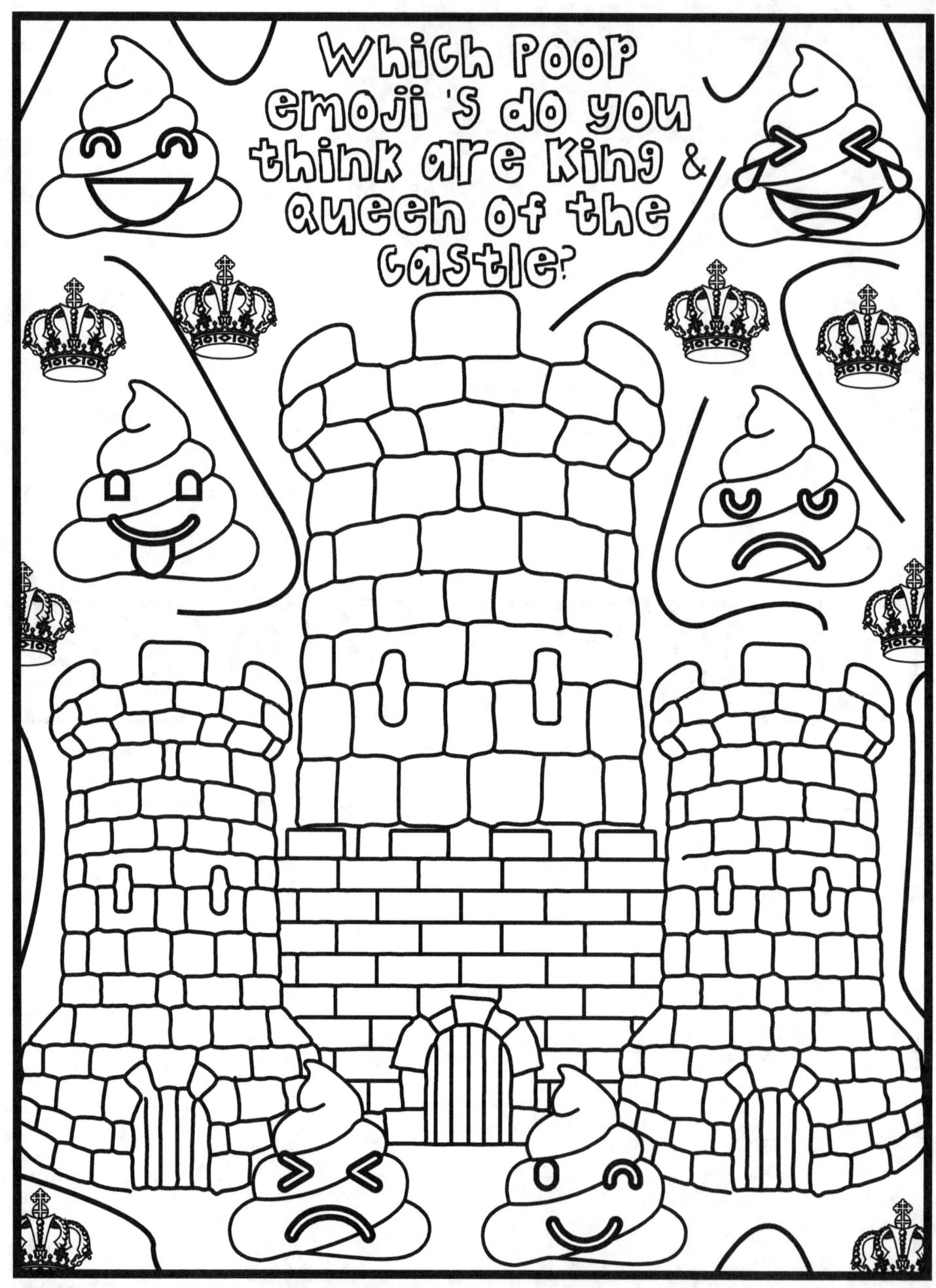

BLEED PAGE

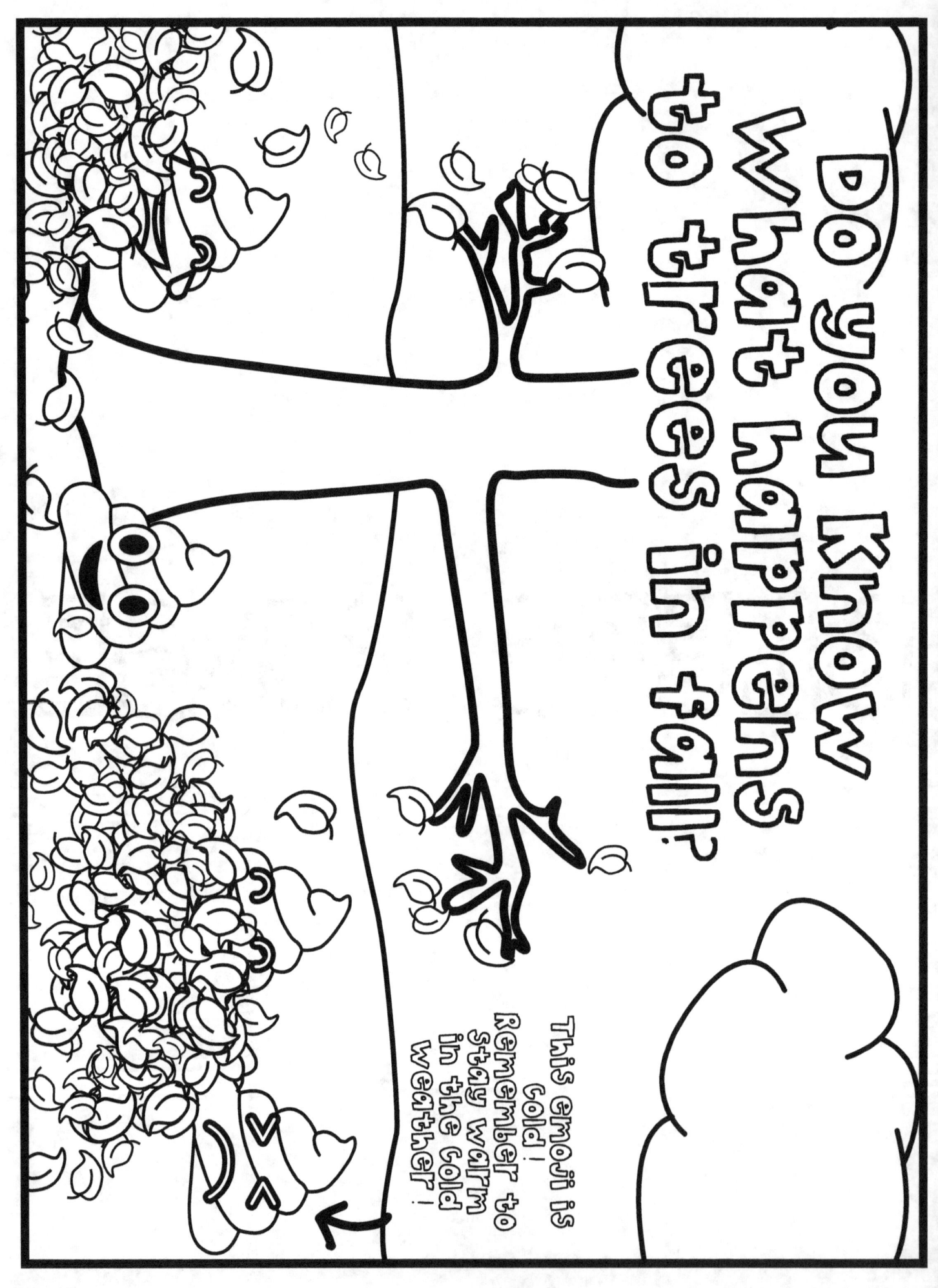

BLEED PAGE

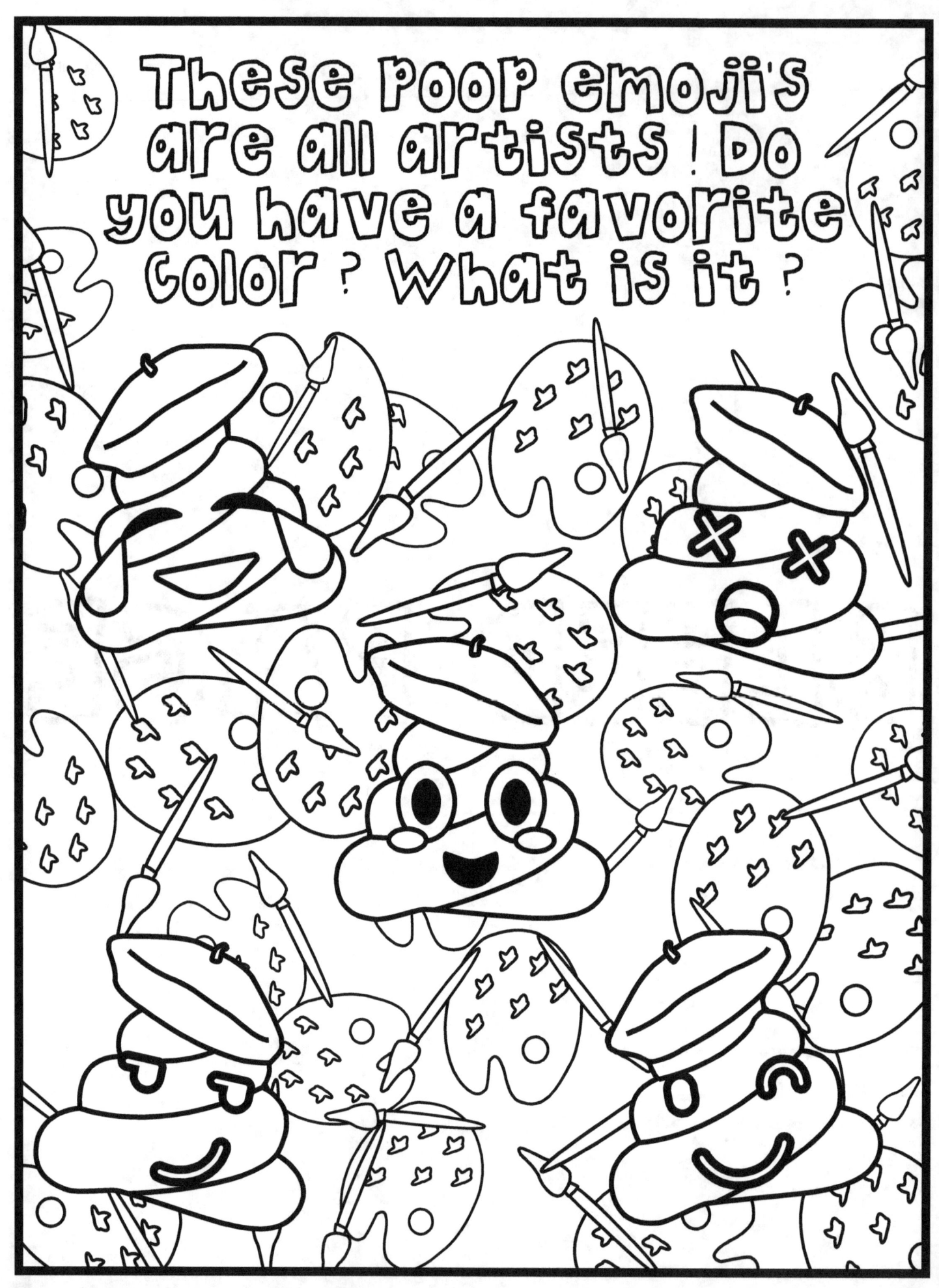

BLEED PAGE

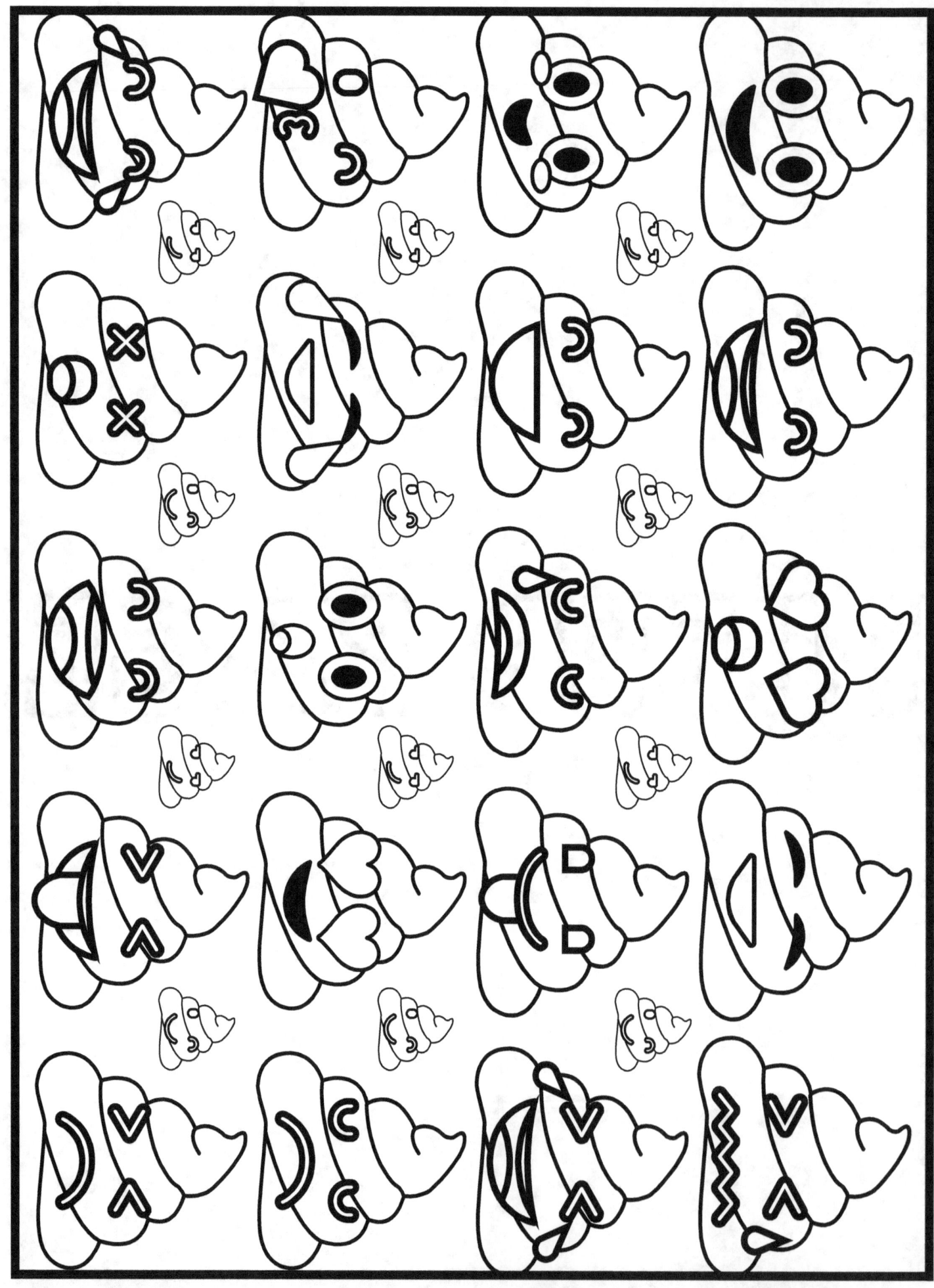

BLEED PAGE

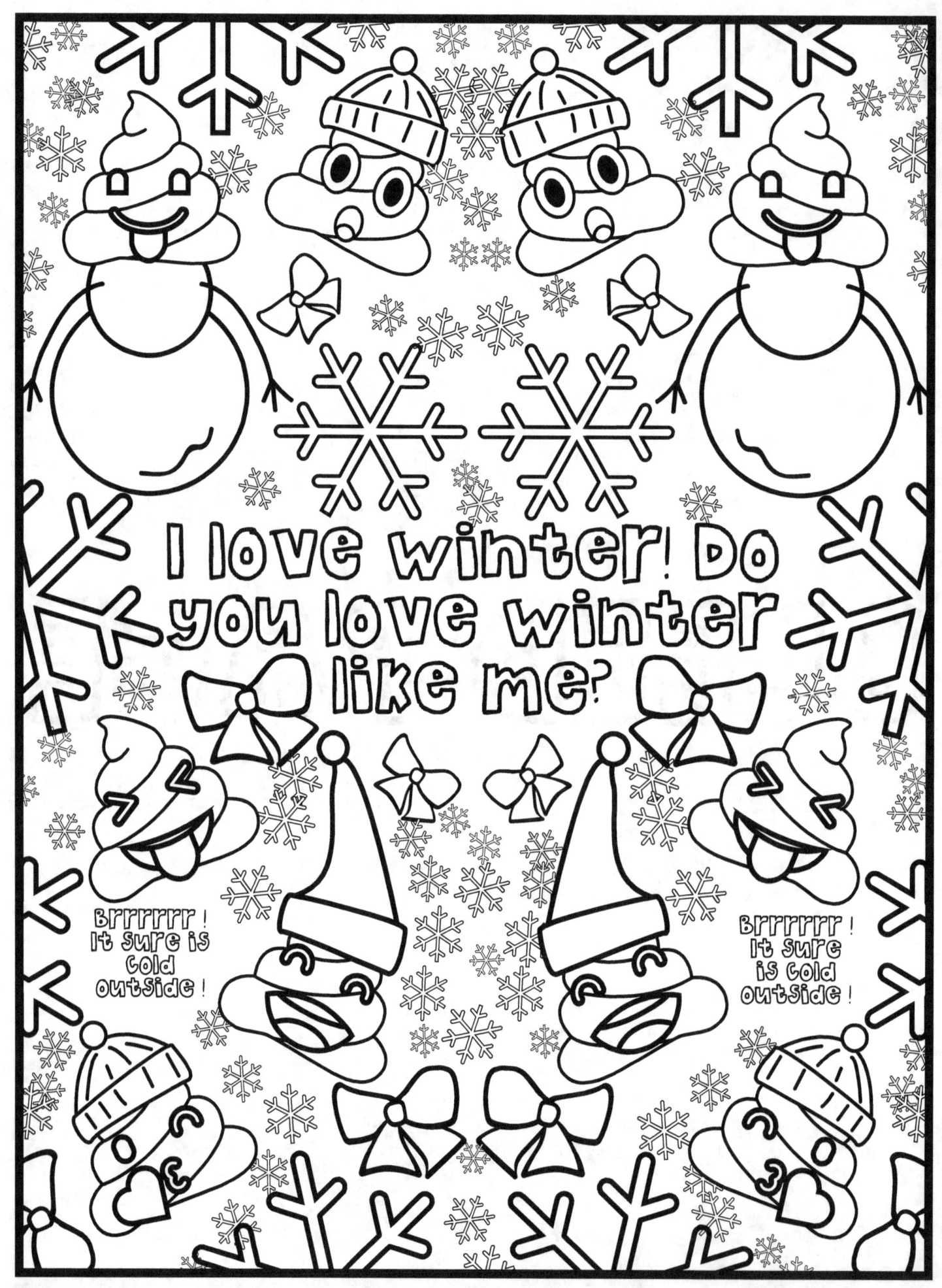

BLEED PAGE

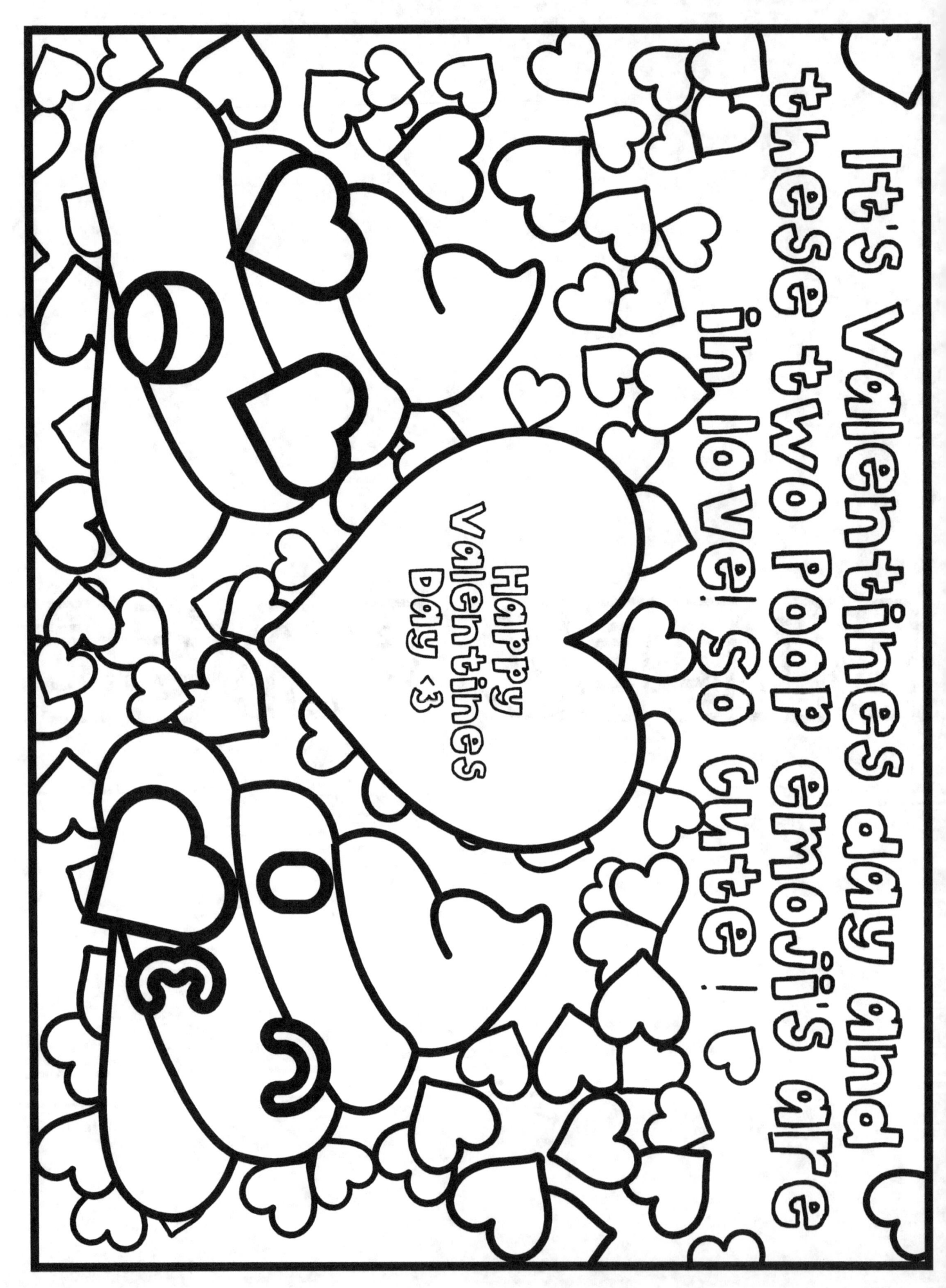

It's Valentines day and these two poop emoji's are in love! So cute!

Happy Valentines Day <3

BLEED PAGE

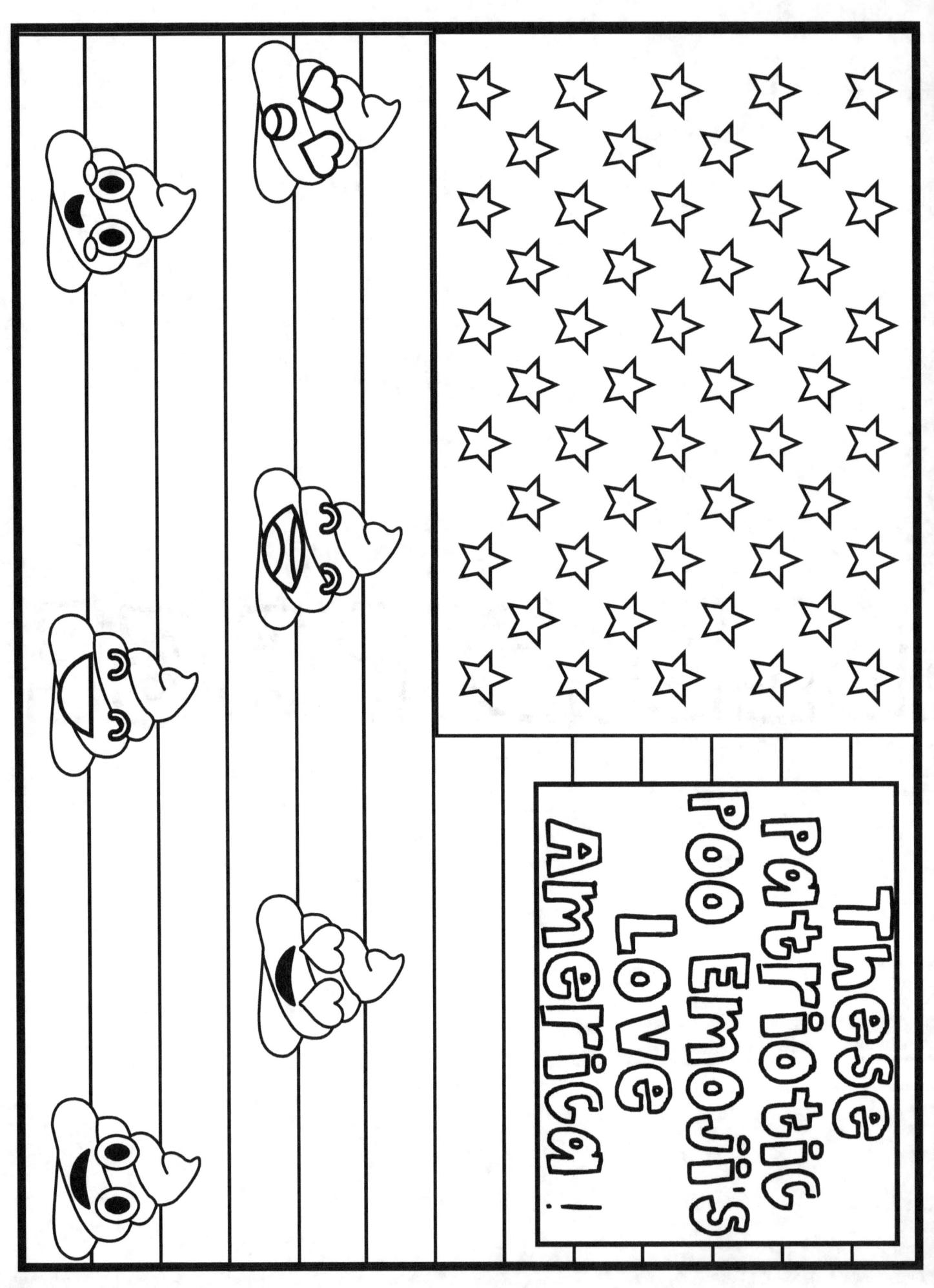

BLEED PAGE

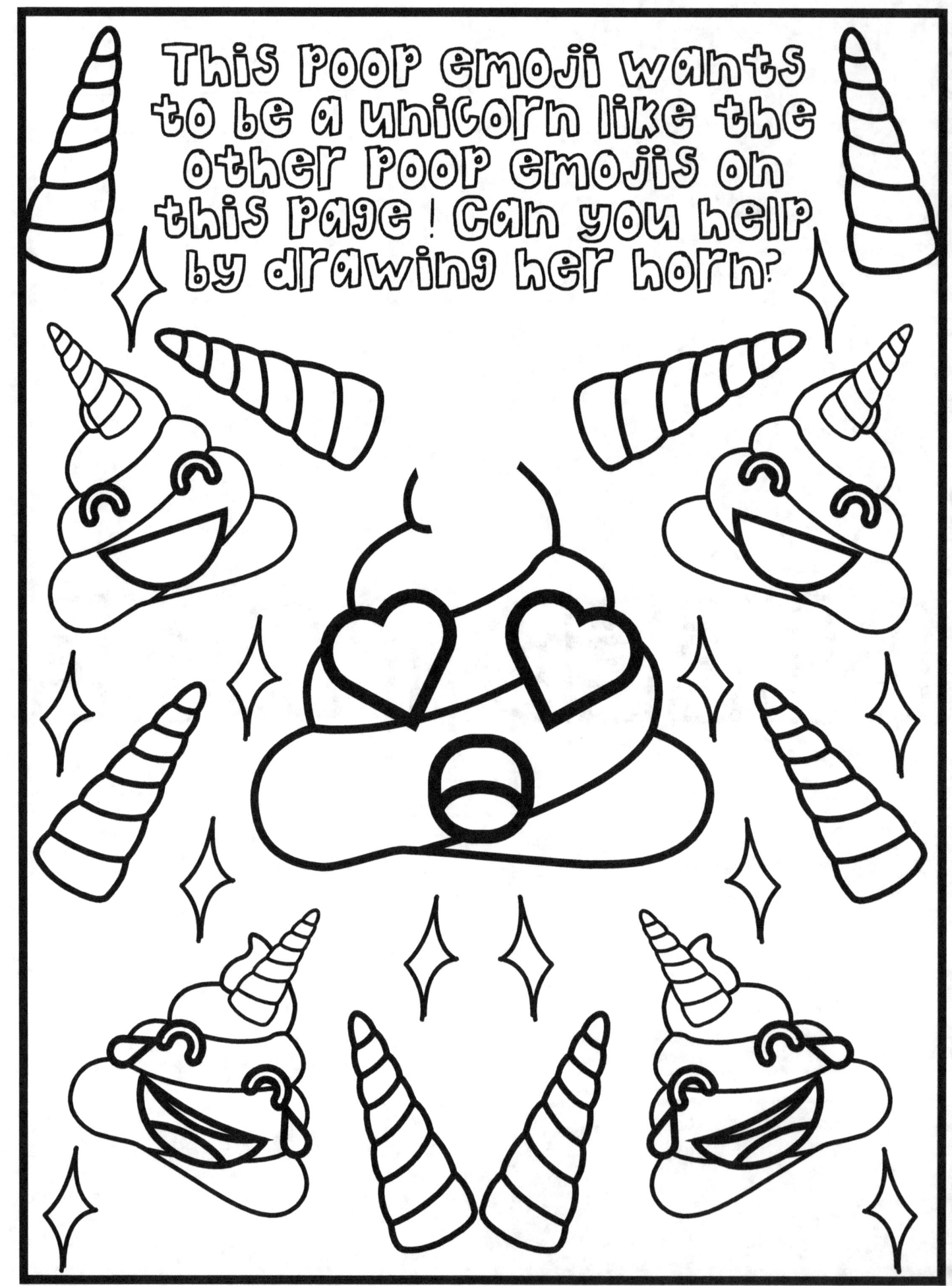

BLEED PAGE

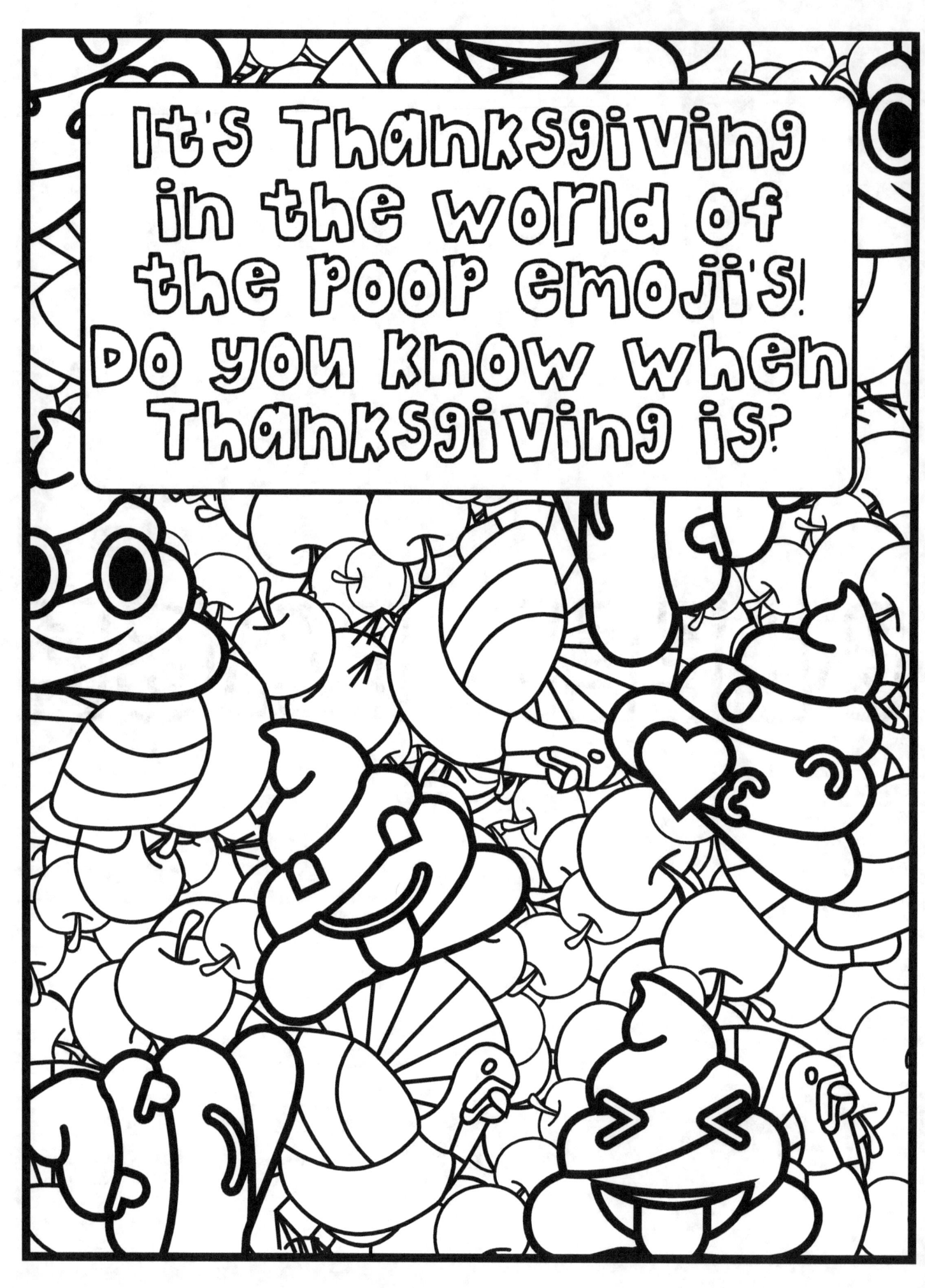

BLEED PAGE

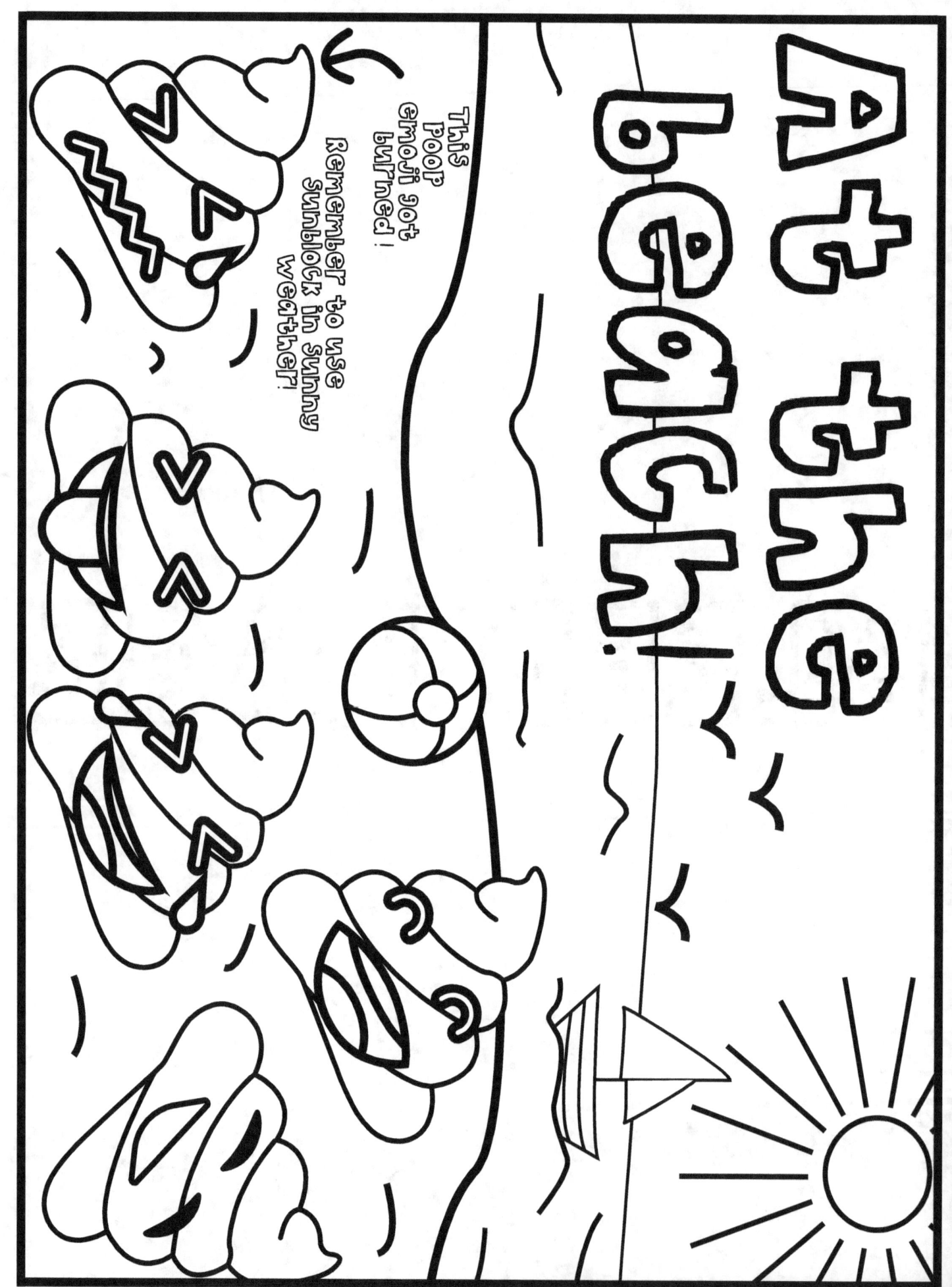

BLEED PAGE

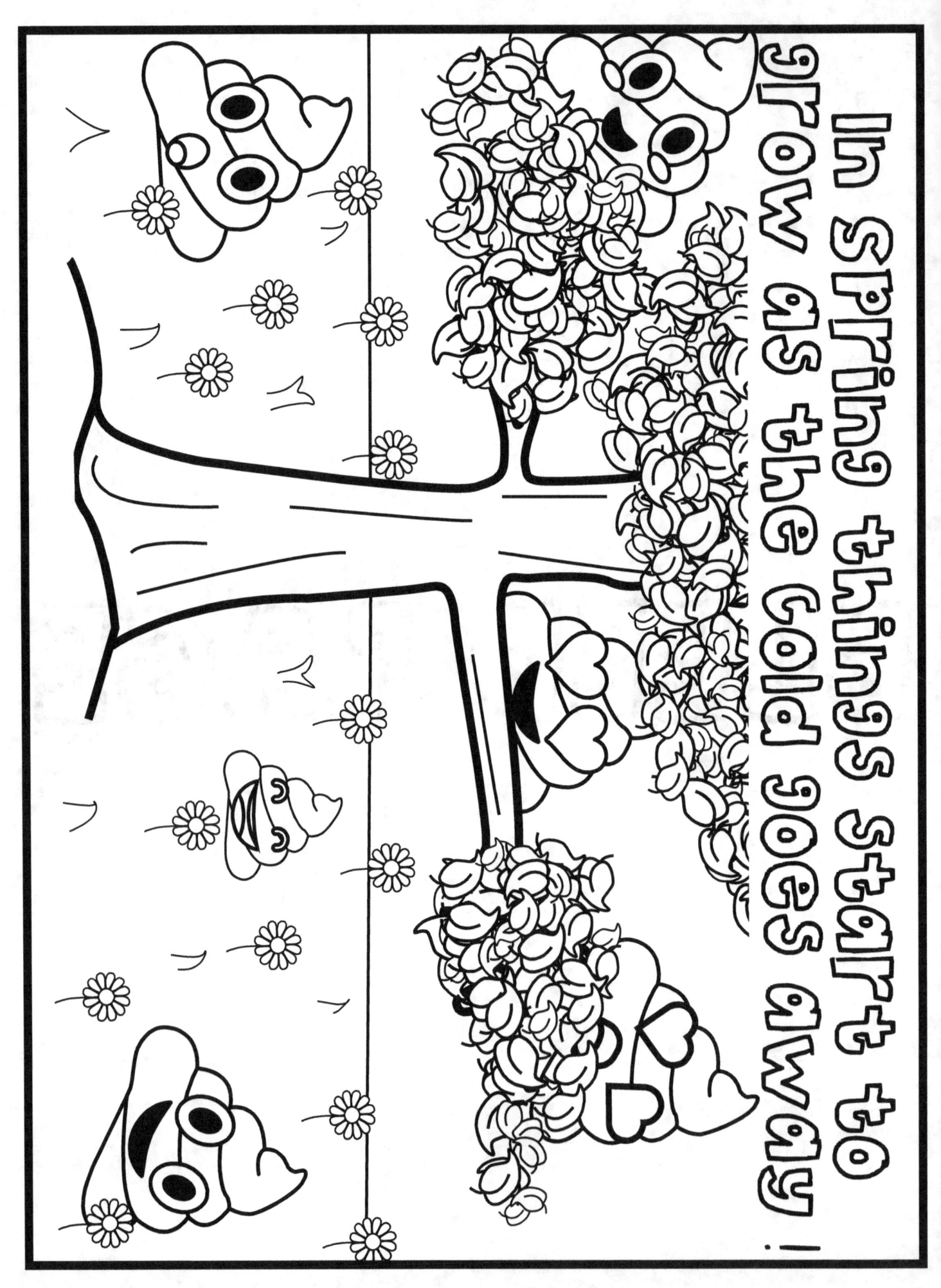

In spring things start to grow as the cold goes away!

BLEED PAGE

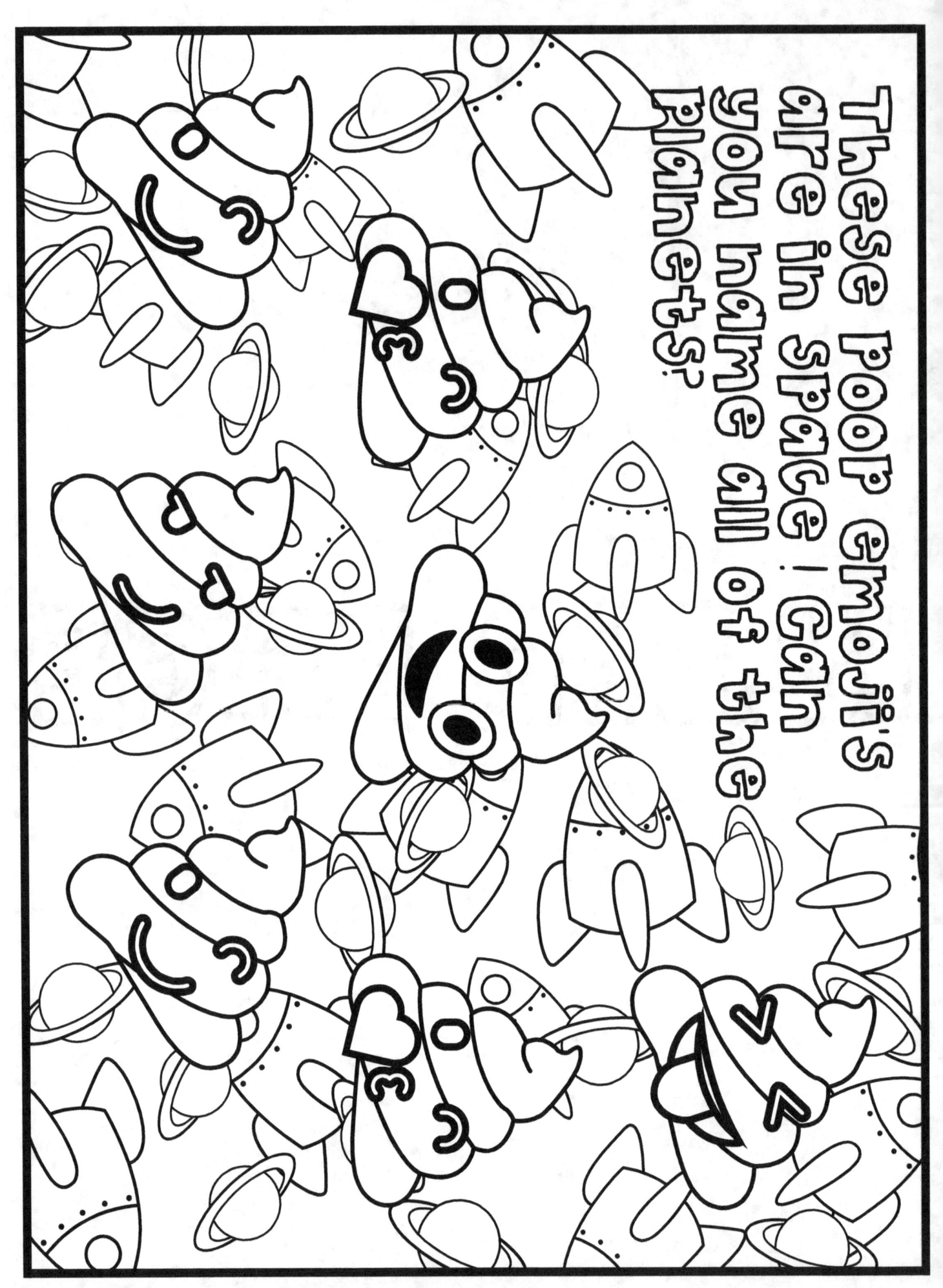

BLEED PAGE

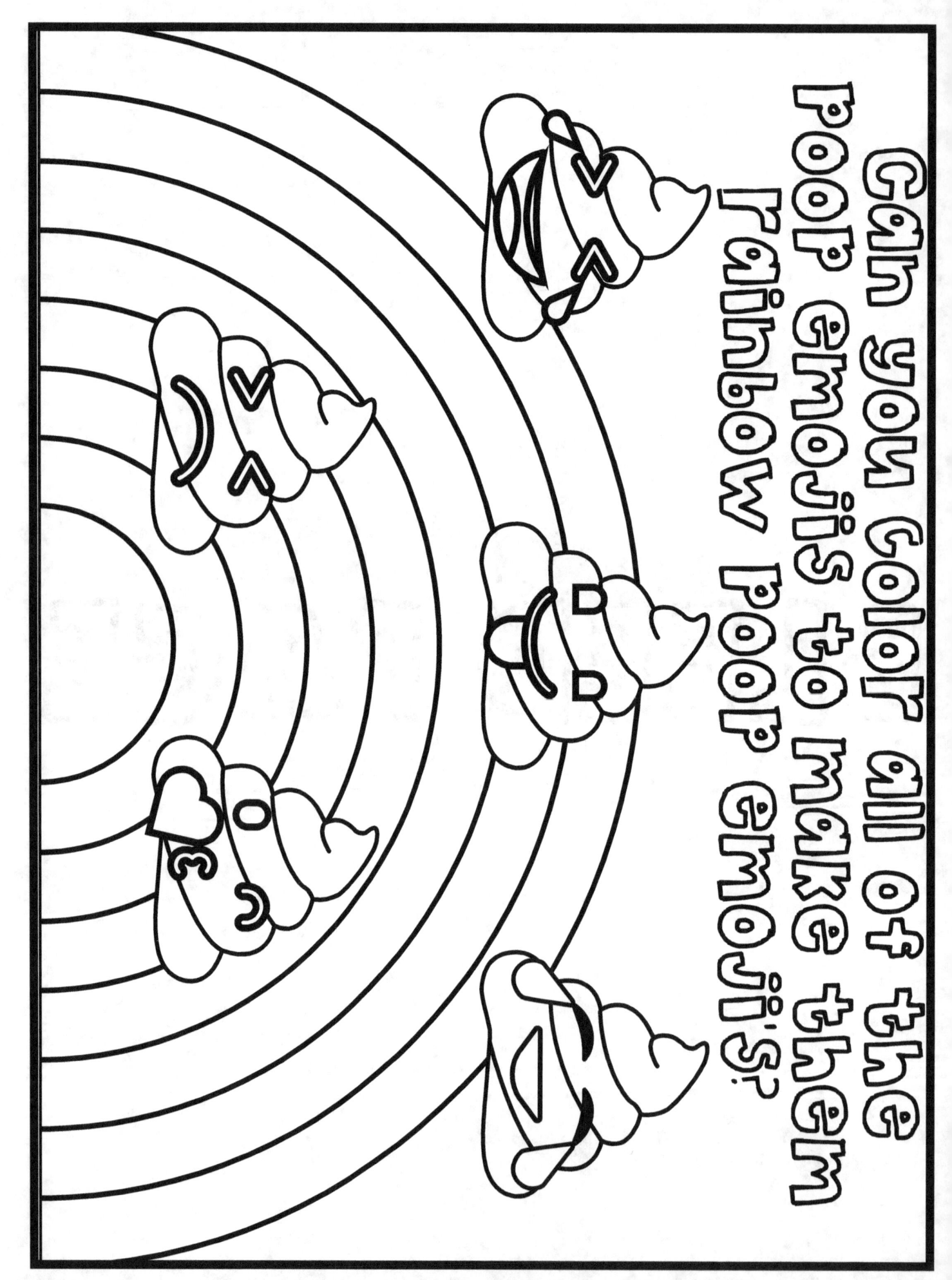

BLEED PAGE

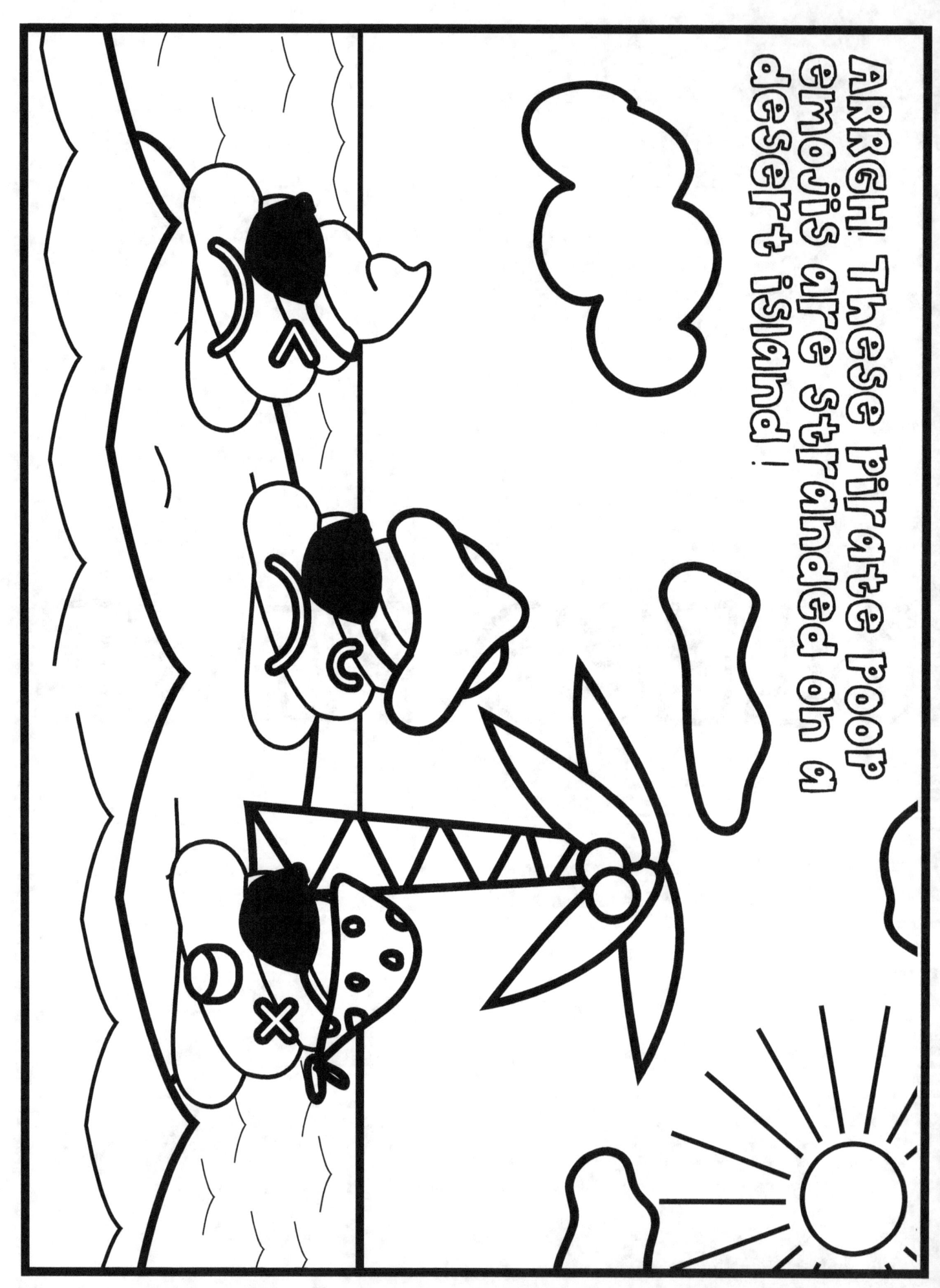

BLEED PAGE

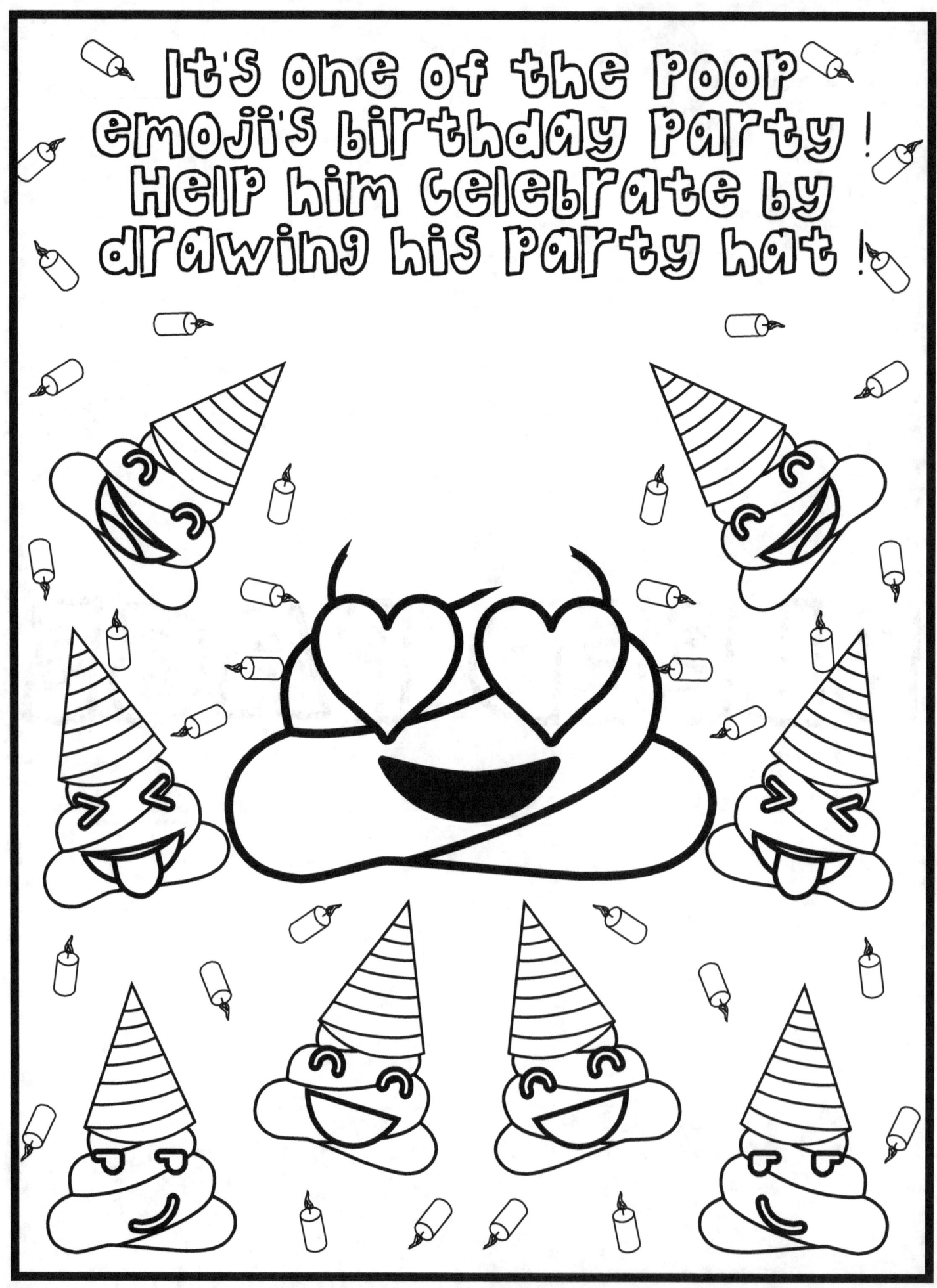

BLEED PAGE

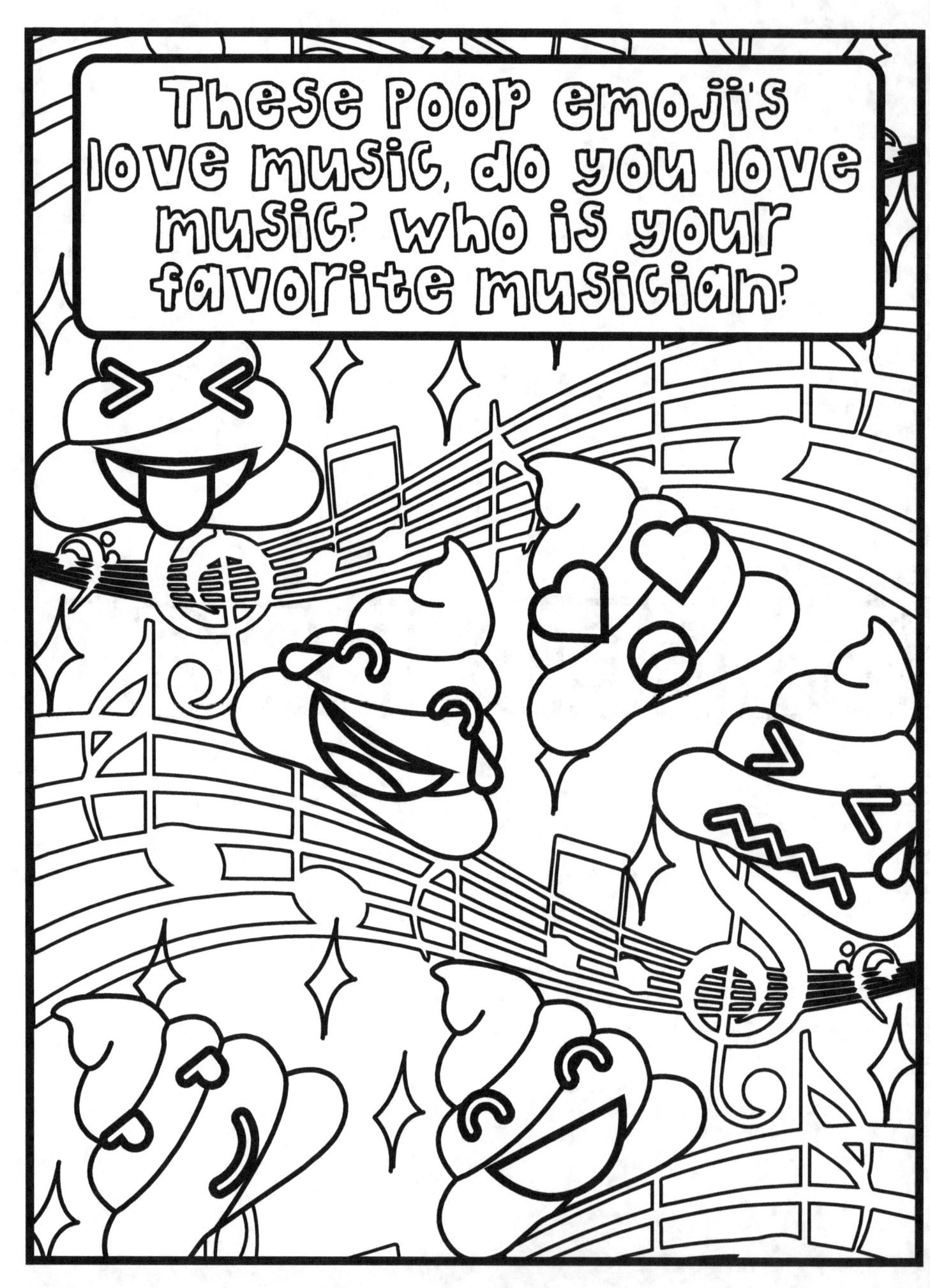

BLEED PAGE

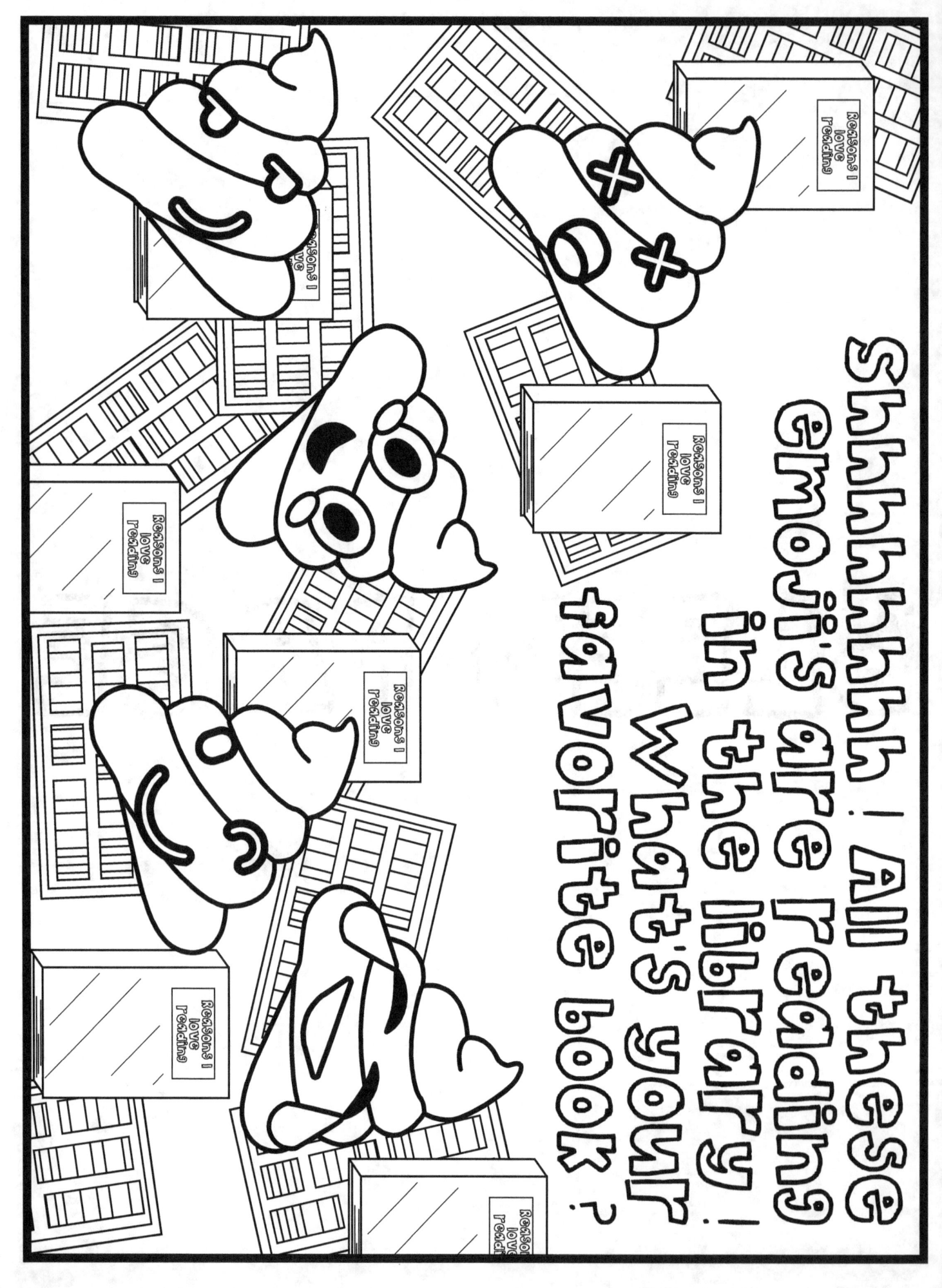

Shhhhhhh! All these emoji's are reading in the library! What's your favorite book?

BLEED PAGE

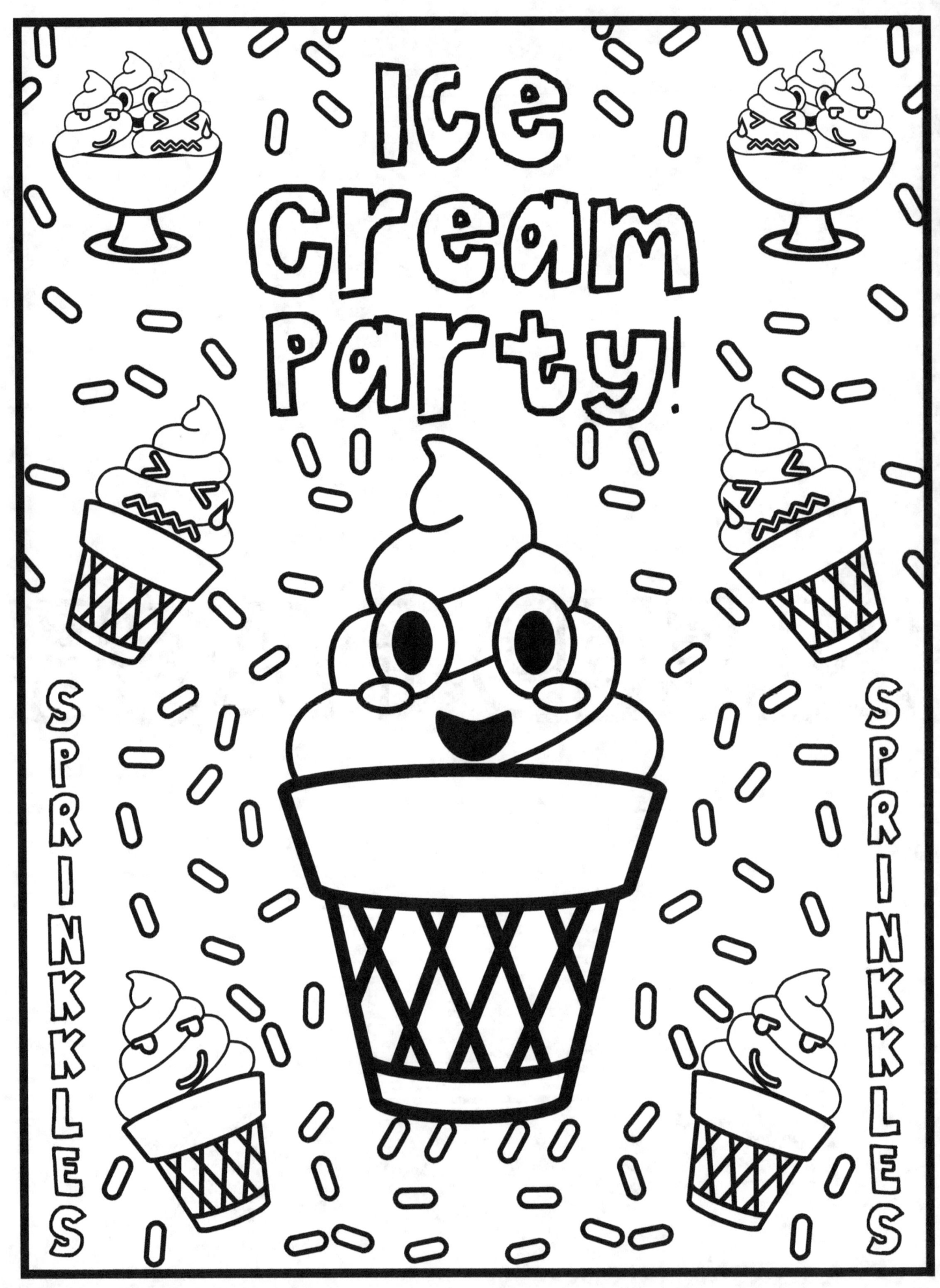

BLEED PAGE

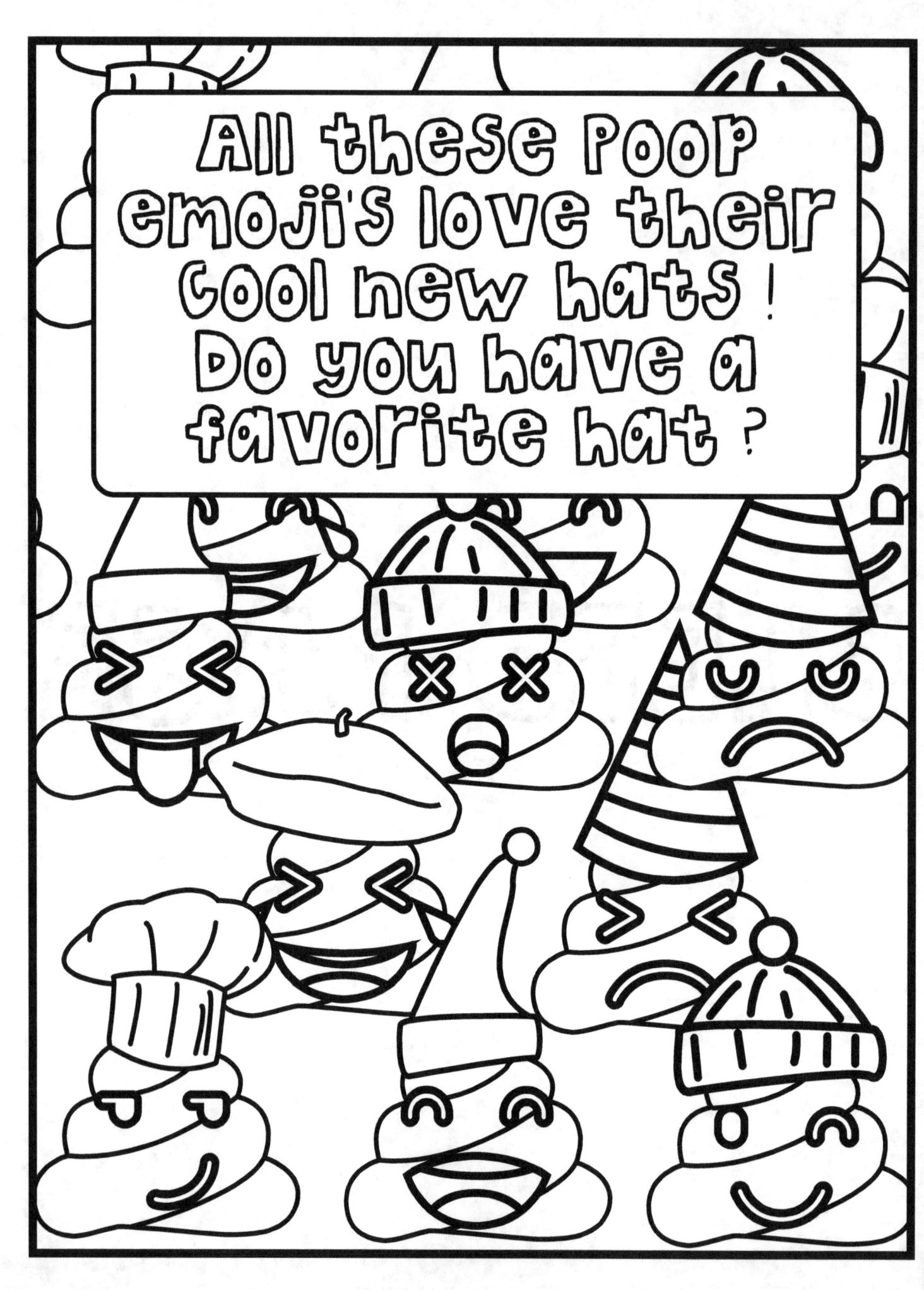

BLEED PAGE

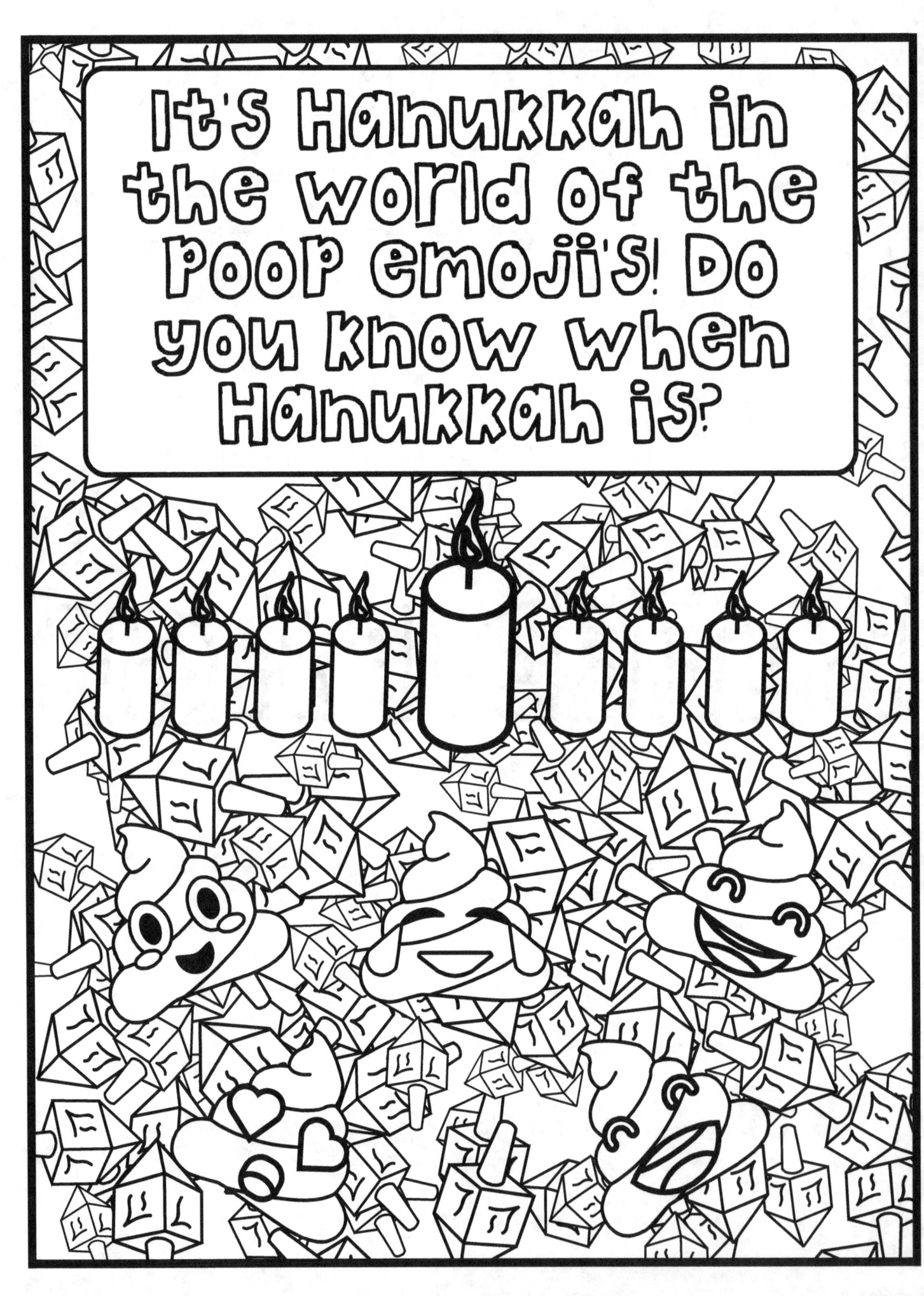

BLEED PAGE

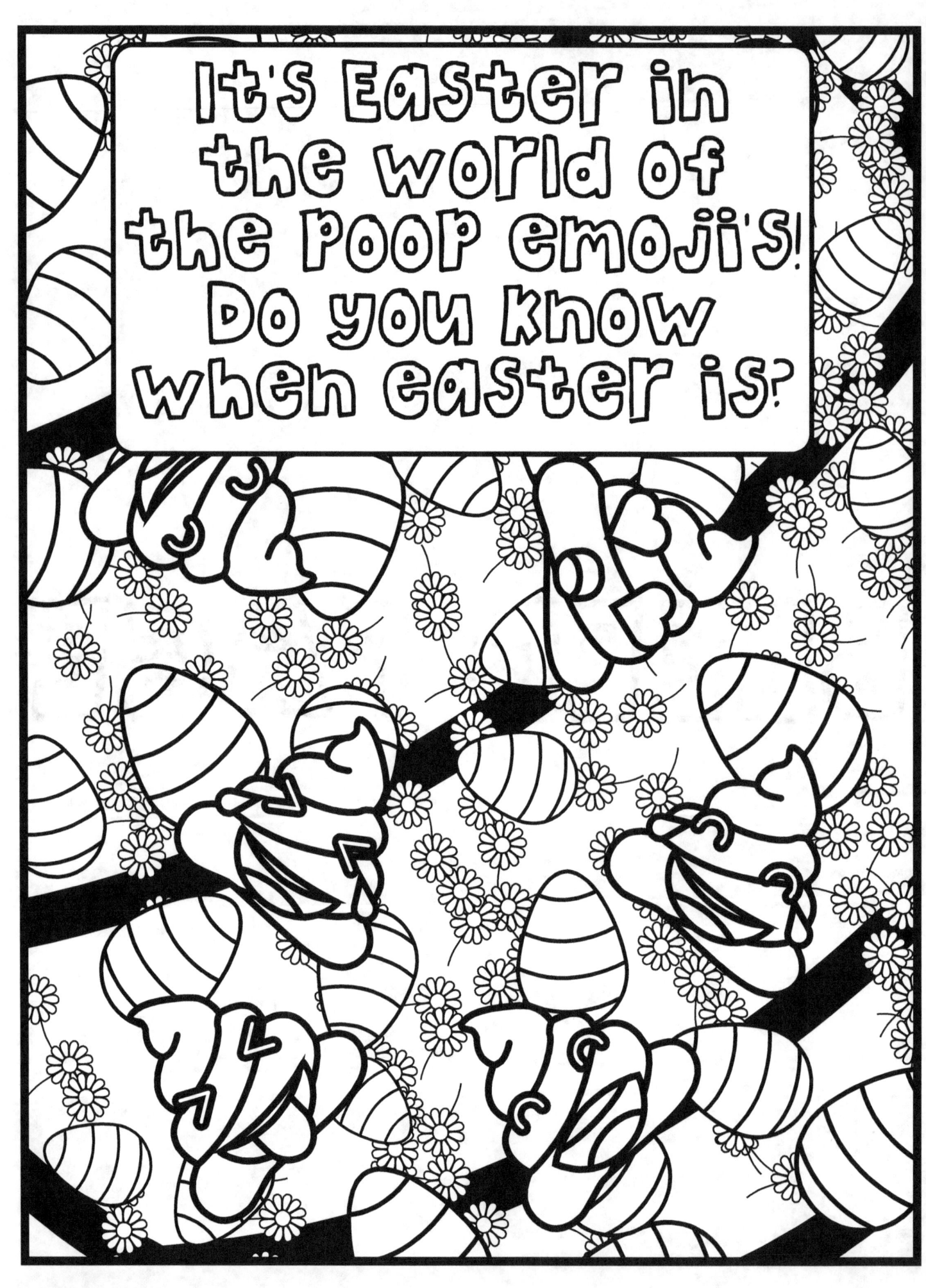

BLEED PAGE

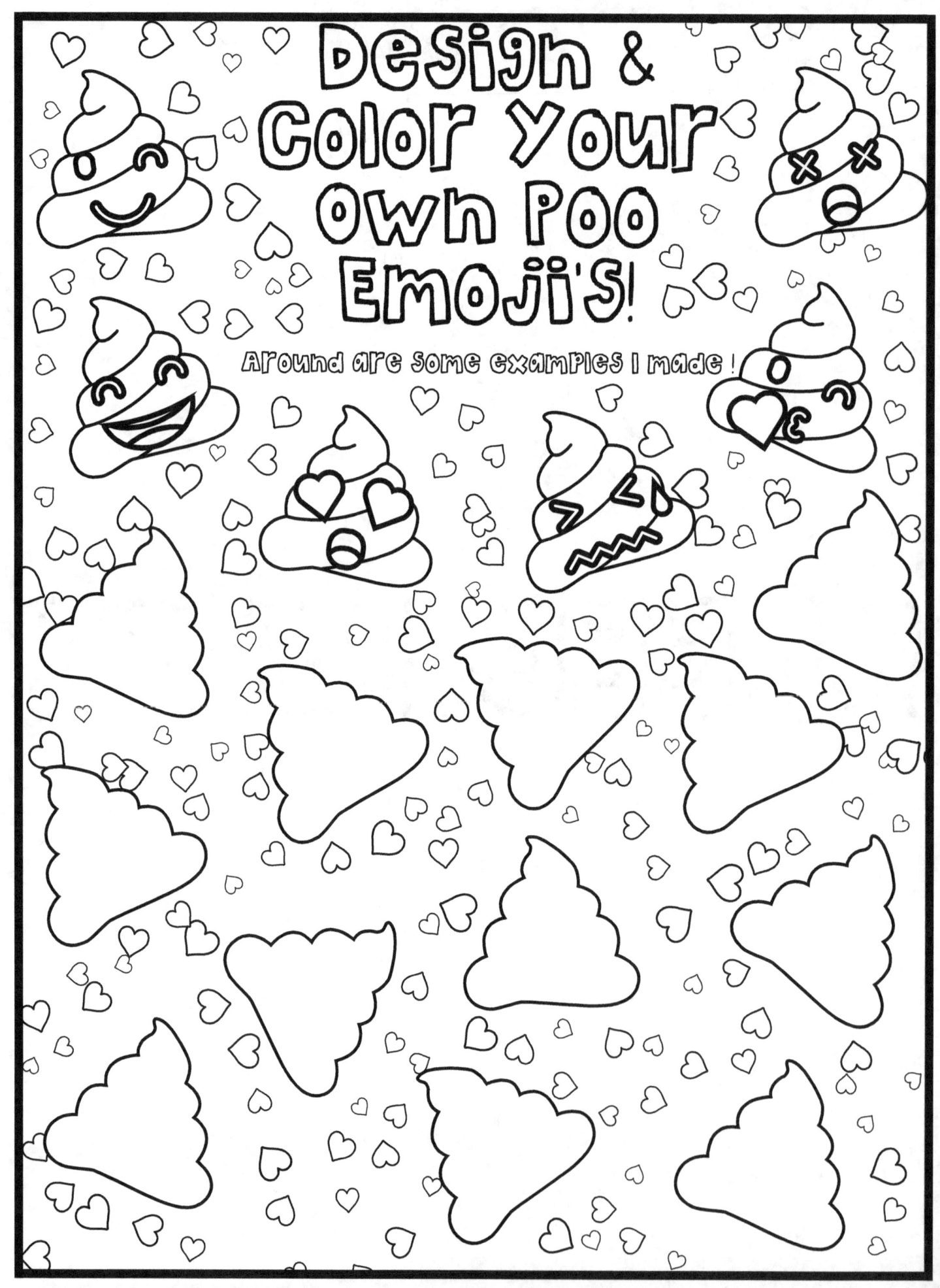

Design & Color Your Own Poo Emoji's!

Around are some examples I made!

BLEED PAGE

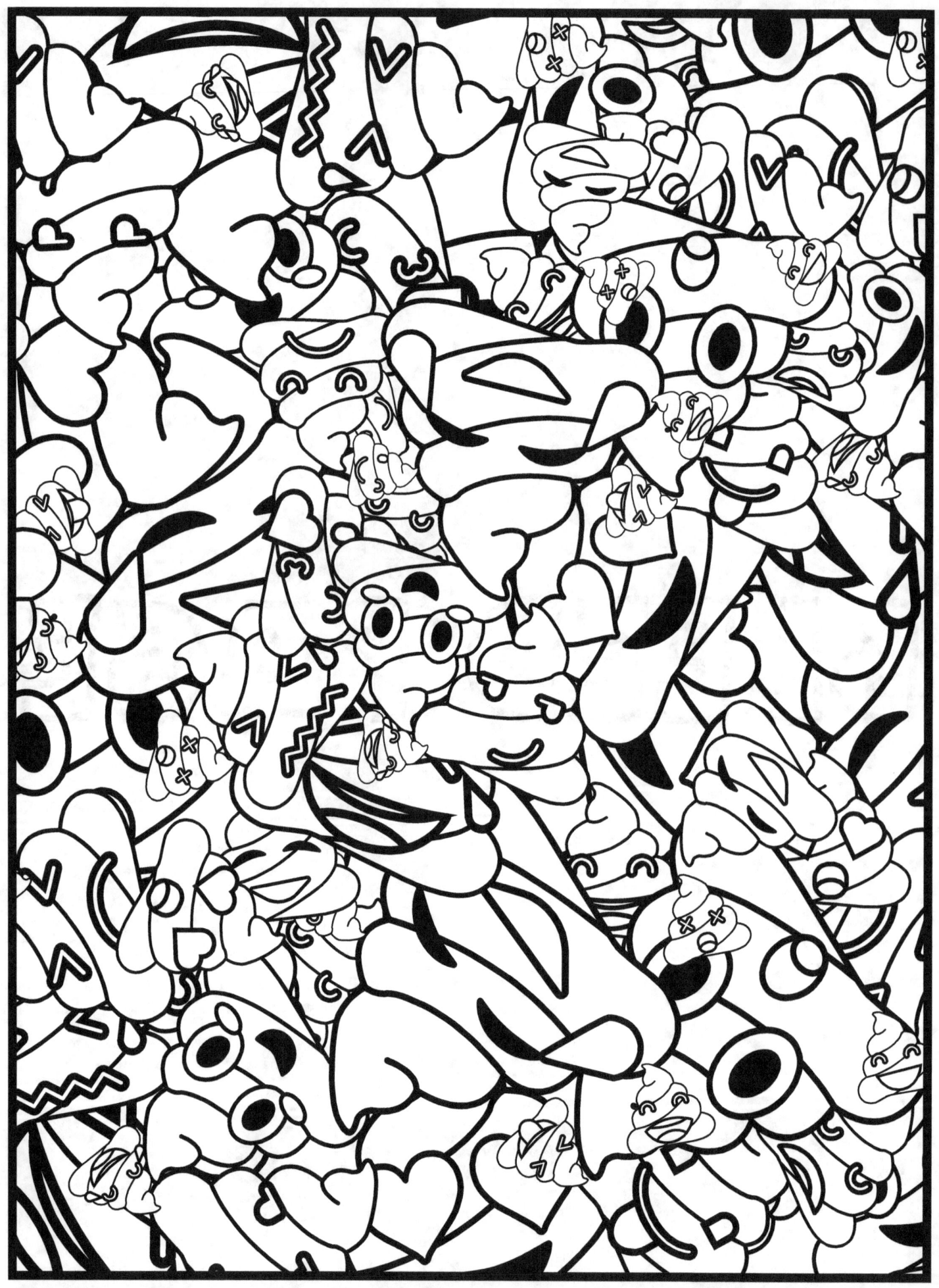

BLEED PAGE

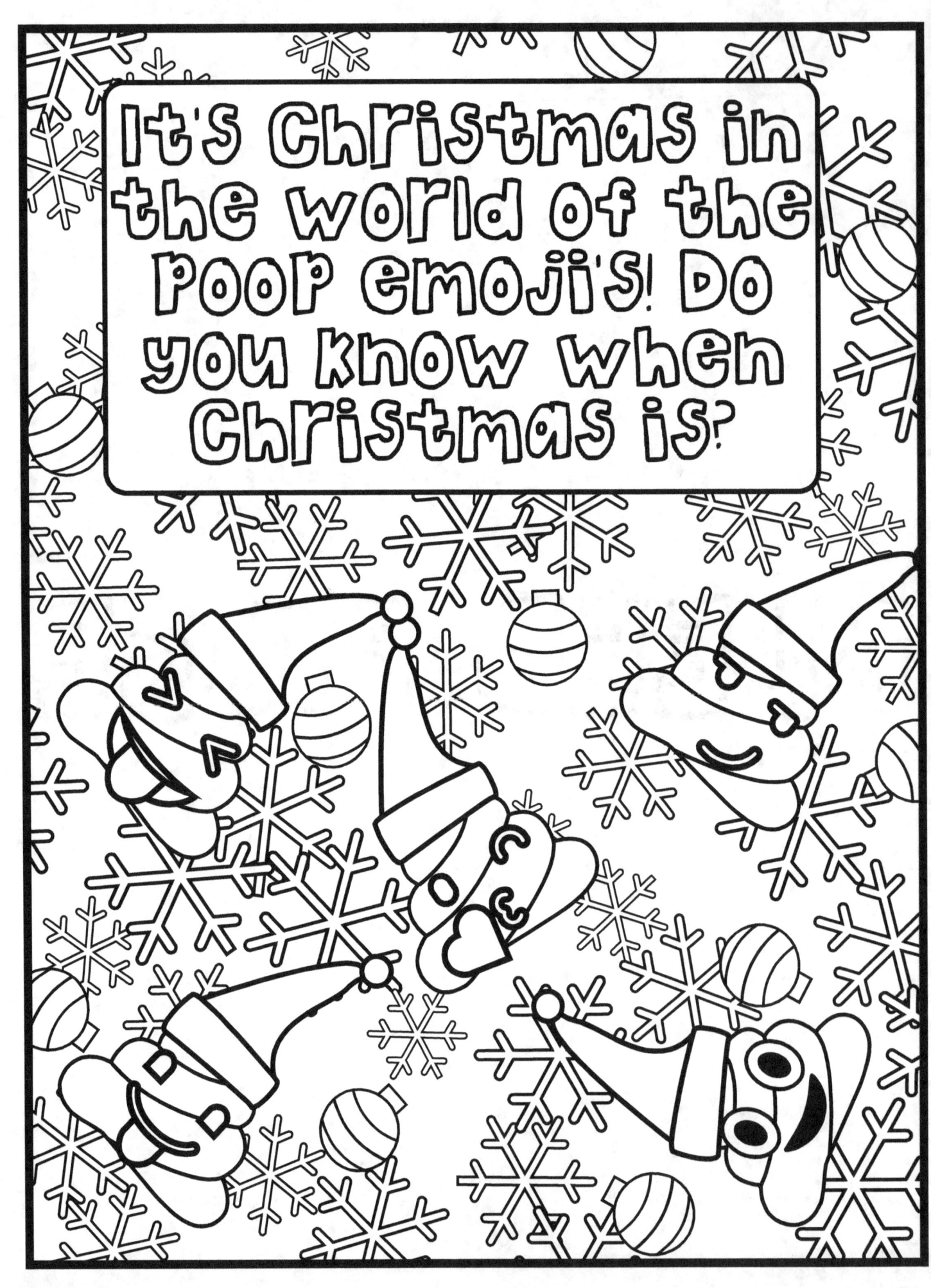

BLEED PAGE

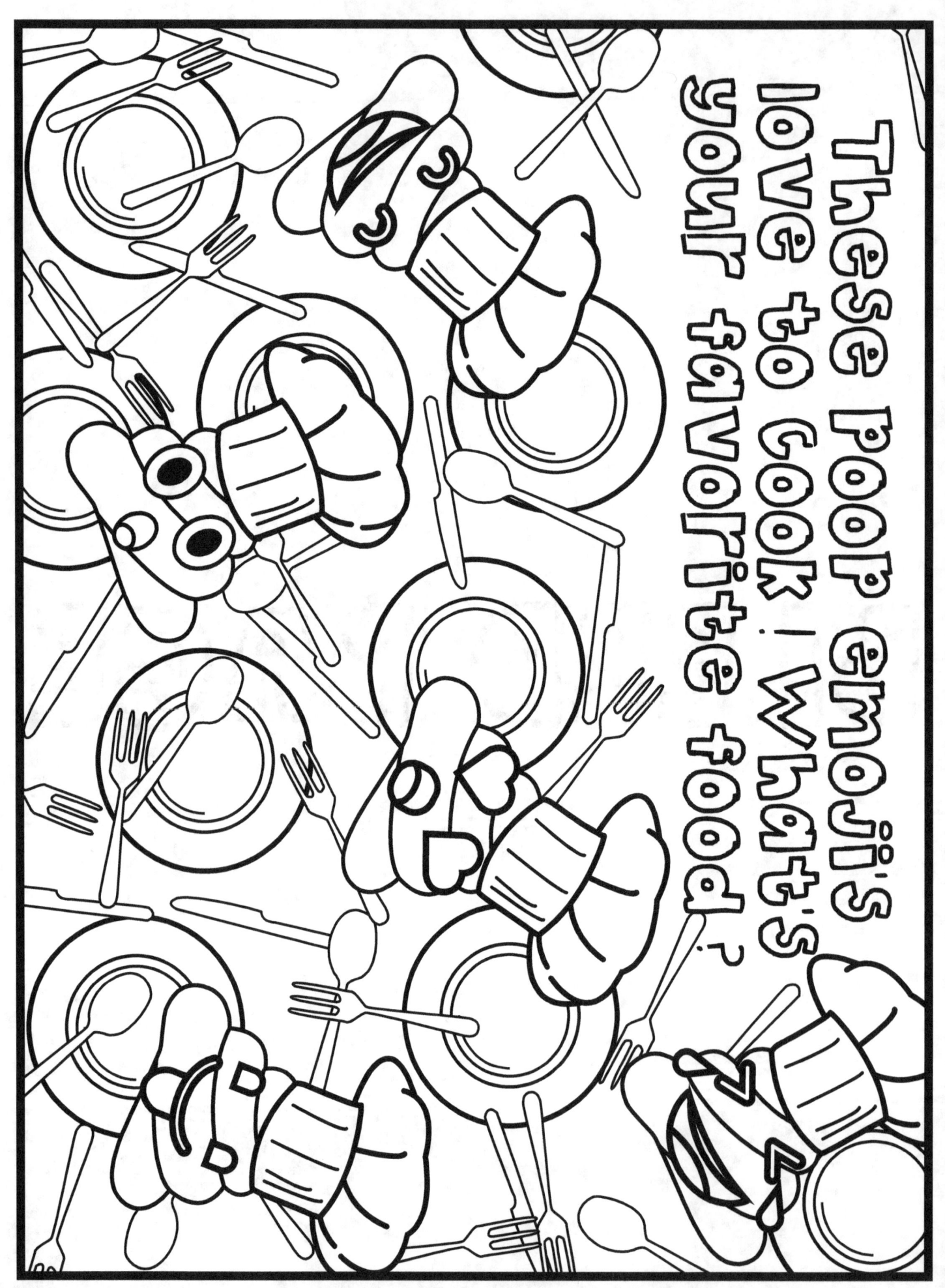

BLEED PAGE

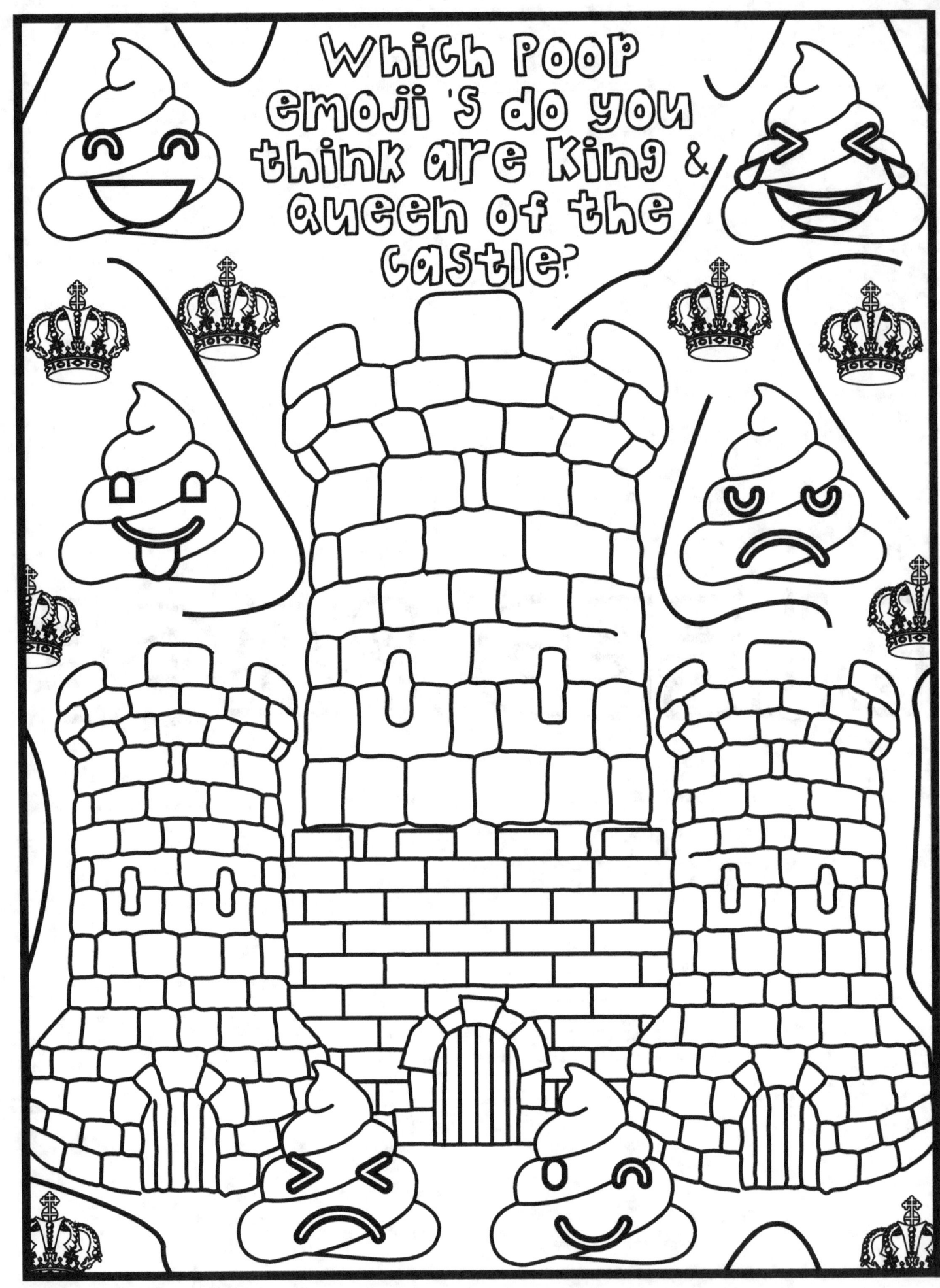

BLEED PAGE

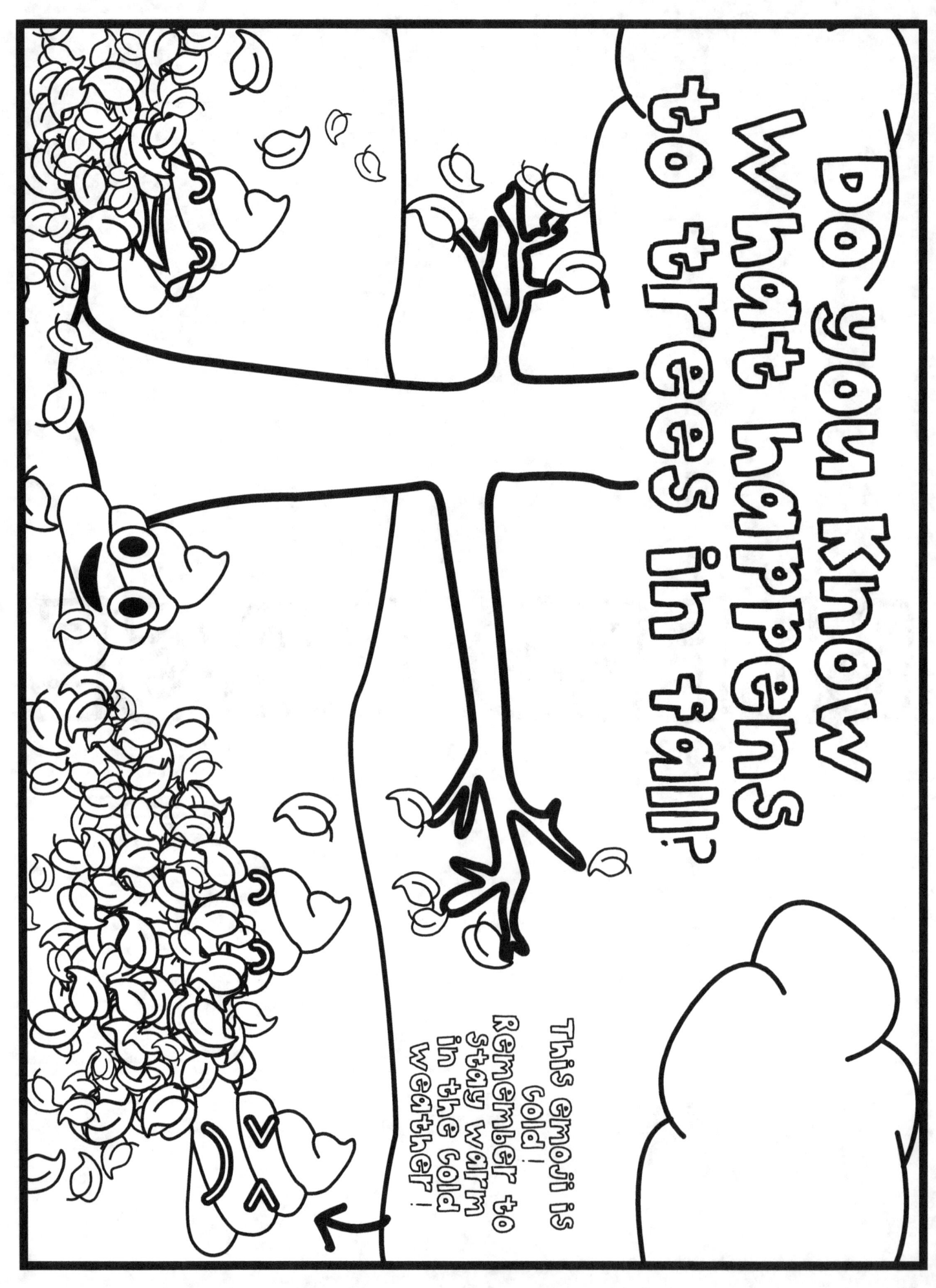

BLEED PAGE

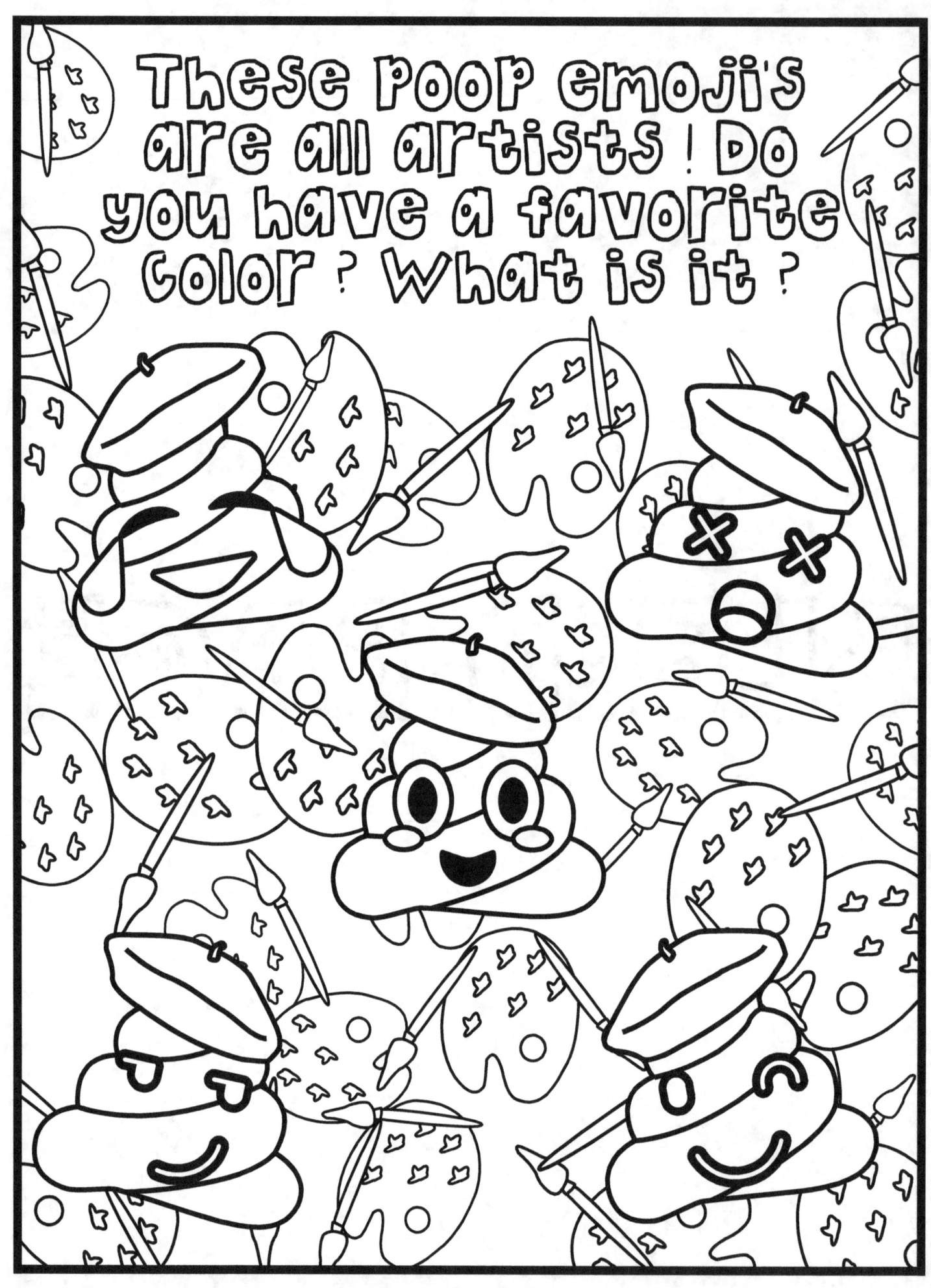

BLEED PAGE

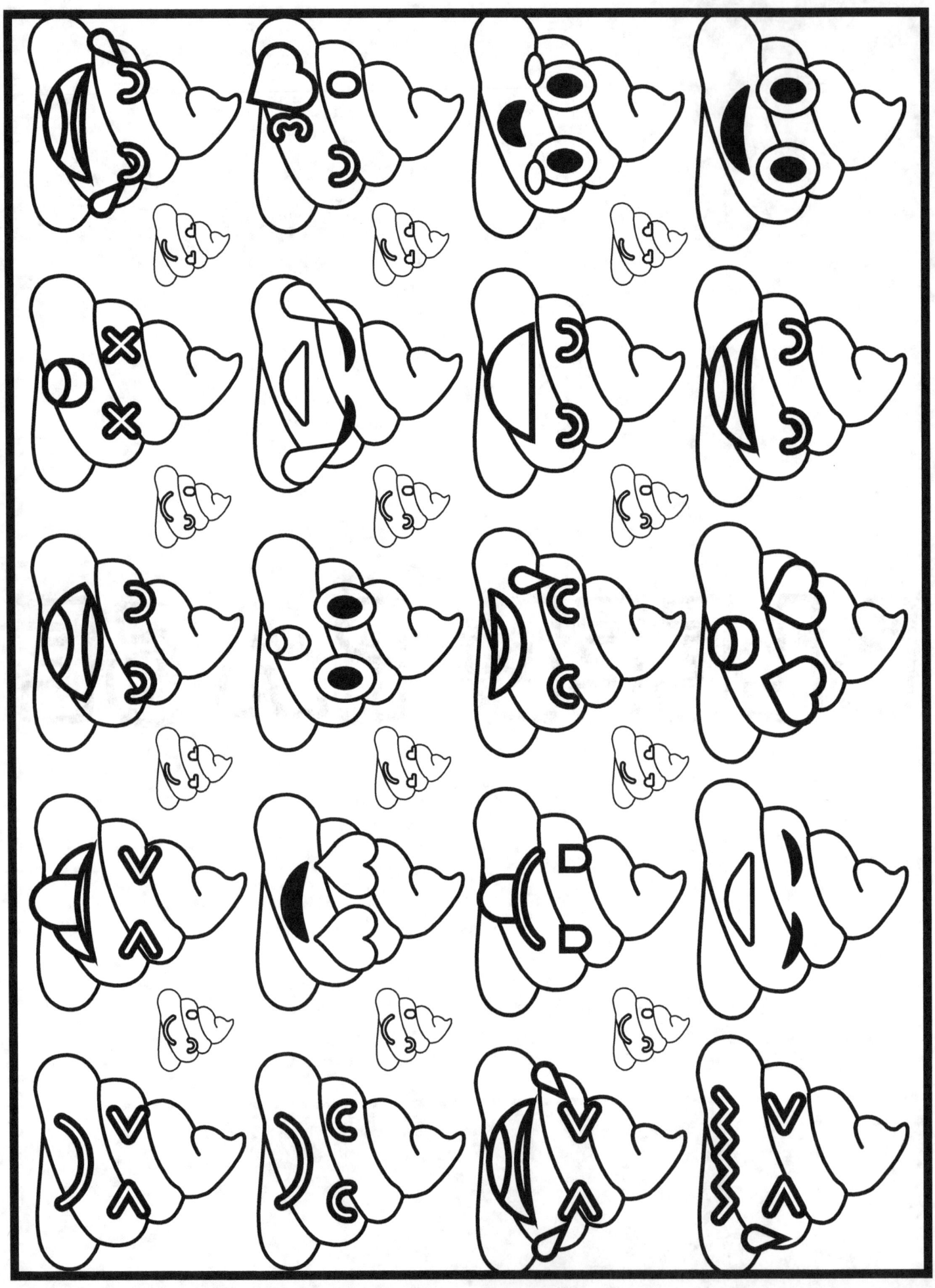

BLEED PAGE

www.ingramcontent.com/pod-product-compliance
Lightning Source LLC
Chambersburg PA
CBHW081605220526

45468CB00010B/2782